Praise for
Moving a Relative & Other Transi~~t~~

Laurie White and Beth Spencer have come up with yet another helpful guide for those living with and caring for loved ones with dementia. *Moving a Relative and Other Transitions in Dementia Care* takes on some of the most challenging situations and decisions that family members face. The authors have gathered sage advice from the leader experts in the field to help make the journey easier. They address challenges such as getting a diagnosis, learning how to live well after diagnosis, tackling issues with driving and safety and, finding the best quality care, support and living arrangements. Everyone who's been diagnosed with dementia wants to live life to the fullest and preserve their dignity and well-being. This book shares insights on how to make that desired outcome a reality.

>   -Elizabeth Edgerly, PhD, Executive Director, Alzheimer's Association, Northern California and Northern Nevada Chapter

Every family should receive *Moving a Relative and Other Transitions in Dementia Care* at the time of a dementia diagnosis. When my husband Bill began his journey with Fronto-Temporal Dementia, the content of this book would have been invaluable. Laurie White and Beth Spencer have provided a complete picture of what to consider, bolstered by case studies and where to go for additional information. All of this is packaged in a user-friendly, easy to digest manner. I definitely recommend it to anyone touched by this disease.

>   -Patt Martin, Experienced Caregiver, Dementia Advocate, and Volunteer Dementia Educator

Moving a Relative and Other Transitions in Dementia Care is a well written easy-to-understand book for dementia caregivers. I wish I had this book available to me when I was faced with the decision to place my wife in a memory care residential facility and all the emotions that came along with moving her out of our home. As a caregiver and a support group facilitator for young-onset dementia caregivers, I recommend this book to any caregiver in need of advice for moving their loved one.

>   - Jon Lucas: family caregiver, support group facilitator,
>   Alzheimer's disease Congressional advocate

This guide will help families through a maze of decisions when a loved one must move to a new home. It's written in simple and practical terms, reflecting the two authors' long experience with helping families through this difficult process.

>   -Daniel Kuhn, national speaker, author and Vice President of Education, All Trust Home Care

As a care partner for someone living with dementia, my life is full. I am grateful to Laurie White and Beth Spencer for *Transitions in Dementia Care*, a book that does not read like a text book, but as a guide book. Its easily accessible language, examples of case studies, and links to additional resources allow me to pick and choose information that I might need at a particular moment in time. Change is difficult, takes effort, and oftentimes makes life messier before it makes life better. With this in mind, I am thankful for the snippets of guidance and encouragement provided in this book for help along the way.

>   -Patricia Cox, Care Partner

ISBN: 9781795079938

Front cover and book design by Tillie Spencer
www.tilliespencer.com

Published by Dementia Care Books
www.dementiacarebooks.com
books@dementiacarebooks.com

First printing 2019

MOVING A RELATIVE
& OTHER TRANSITIONS
IN DEMENTIA CARE

Laurie White

Beth Spencer

Contents

.....

WITH LOVE AND THANKS TO

Tom White
Copy Editor

Tillie Spencer
Graphic Designer

This handbook is dedicated
to the many hundreds of family members we have had the privilege of
working with over the past thirty-plus years.

ABOUT THE AUTHORS

Laurie White, MSW, and Beth Spencer, MSW, MA, have worked in the field of dementia care for over 30 years. They met on the board of the Alzheimer's Association in 1984 and began working together in 1988 in their private counseling and care management practice in Ann Arbor, Michigan. Throughout their careers, they have worked with family caregivers and people with dementia in residential, medical and educational settings, adult day programs, and support groups for both care partners and people with memory loss. Both Laurie and Beth have presented information on dementia related topics at national and regional conferences and have conducted training programs for professionals who work in a variety of settings. Beth and Laurie are the authors of *Coping with Behavior Change in Dementia*, which discusses causes and strategies for understanding a number of the behavioral issues that arise in dementia. *Moving a Relative with Memory Loss*, now out of print, was first published in 2000.

Laurie lives in Santa Rosa, California, and Beth is in Ann Arbor, Michigan.

More about the authors and book ordering information are available at:
dementiacarebooks.com

CONTRIBUTORS

Nancy Barbas, MD, MSW, is Emeritus Associate Professor of Neurology at Michigan Medicine, Ann Arbor, Michigan where she served as Director of the Cognitive Disorder Clinic for 12 years and continues as member of the Executive Committee and consultant to the Michigan Alzheimer's Disease Center. She takes great pleasure in teaching the next generation of physicians at the University of Michigan in courses on Doctoring and Medical Humanities.

Ruth Gay, MS, has worked for the Alzheimer's Association for 21 years. She is currently the Chief Public Policy Officer for the Alzheimer's Association of Northern California and Northern Nevada. As an expert on the issues of policy gaps and service delivery for people with Alzheimer's disease and other dementias, Ruth directs the Federal Policy and Advocacy efforts as well as State Policy Strategic Planning for Northern California and Nevada.

Mariana Longoria Ibarrola, MD, is Atlantic Fellow for Equity in Brain Health, Memory and Aging Center, University of California San Francisco in the Cognitive Aging and Dementia Department. She is also part of the Psychiatry Department at the National Institute of Neurology and Neurosurgery of Mexico.

Daniel Kuhn, MSW, is Vice President of Education at All Trust Home Care that primarily serves people with dementia living in the Chicago area. For more than 40 years he has been a licensed clinical social worker in various care and research settings including the Rush Alzheimer's Disease Center, the Alzheimer's Association, and Rainbow Hospice and Palliative Care. He has authored or co-authored more than 50 publications including *Alzheimer's Early Stages: First Steps for Family, Friends and Caregivers.*
He can be reached at dan@alltrusthomecare.com.

Grace Lee, LCSW, ACSW, is a Geriatric Case Manager at the Senior Health and Memory Center, Kaiser Permanente Santa Clara Medical Center in northern California. She has served on the board of the Alzheimer's Association of Northern California and Northern Nevada and worked at the University of Michigan Geriatrics Center and Alzheimer's Disease Research Center. She has also been a care partner for her mother, Stella, who died from Alzheimer's disease in 2016.

Bruce Miller, MD, is the A.W. & Mary Margaret Clausen Distinguished Professor in Neurology at the University of California, San Francisco. He is also Director of the Memory and Aging Center and Co-Director of the Global Brain Health Institute in the Neurology Department at UCSF.

Janet Thompson, Eldercare Consultant, founded Elder & Family Options to creatively and compassionately work with elders and families to discover options and connect with resources. She has 18 years experience in senior living sales and marketing for continuing care retirement communities, assisted living, memory care, and skilled nursing communities. Janet developed and facilitates a CEU-credentialed program through The Conversation Project which teaches professionals how to have conversations with clients on Advance Care Directives, POLST, and End of Life decisions.

David Troxel, MPH, is a writer, speaker and dementia care consultant based in Sacramento, CA. With Virginia Bell, he is co-author of six influential books including the Best Friends Approach to Dementia Care (Health Professions Press, 2017, second edition). He has been a family care partner to his mother Dorothy who passed away with Alzheimer's disease in 2009. Read more about his work at www.bestfriendsapproach.com and follow him on Facebook at www.facebook.com/bestfriendsapproach.

FOREWORD

Over 5 million Americans have Alzheimer's disease. Millions more have other forms of progressive dementia such as vascular dementia, Lewy Body disease and frontotemporal dementia. Countless others never receive a diagnosis.

As Director of the Michigan Alzheimer's Disease Center and a clinician-scientist who cares for those with dementia, these numbers greatly concern me. Since our population is still aging, and age is the greatest risk factor for developing dementia, the problem will not go away anytime soon. While it's

> **We can't wait for that future. It is imperative, now, that education, support and medical services are provided to the individuals and families coping with dementia today.**

true that promising research is moving us closer to slowing this devastating disease, we still have a long way to go.

We can't wait for that future. It is imperative, now, that education, support and medical services are provided to the individuals and families coping with dementia today. As a neurologist, I've had the privilege of working with many hundreds of patients and families who are living with mild cognitive impairment or dementia. At some point, all of them face challenging decisions regarding daily life. How do we know when a family member with cognitive changes is no longer safe living alone? What should we do when driving becomes a concern? How do we make the decision to move a parent or spouse to assisted living or memory care? This new book by Laurie White and Beth Spencer - *Moving A Relative & Other Transitions in Dementia Care* - will help families navigate these hard decisions.

While researchers continue to search for preventive therapies, health care providers must strive to find better ways to help families through the harsh realities of caring for people with dementia. Every week in the Cognitive Disorders Clinic at the University of Michigan, I see our social workers and nurse practitioners provide continuity and practical expertise to families, offering information about resources and providing an opportunity to discuss the emotional and day-to-day challenges of caregiving. This interdisciplinary approach, I've come to learn, provides the best framework for helping families.

Often, we provide copies of Beth and Laurie's last book, *Coping with Behavior Change in Dementia: A Family Caregiver's Guide,* to families who need help knowing how to respond to the behavioral challenges that can arise during the course of dementia. I've seen the difference it makes for our patients and families. And it's clear why it makes a difference: Beth and Laurie's books are easy to read, practical and serve as a good reference tool.

This new book will be just as useful to families as they take this journey. Beginning with background information on the brain changes that affect decision-making, *Transitions in Dementia Care* helps families understand how decision-making can be impaired in their relatives. It also reviews how and when to get a diagnosis, and why that's important.

A range of tips are provided to help families assess when safety alone becomes a problem. Suggestions for how to find community services and how to convince a reluctant relative to accept them are also included. Several sections address important aspects about making the decision to move a relative with dementia: from the emotional impact of this decision to practical suggestions for finding a place, talking with your relative about it and making the transition as smooth as possible. Other sections discuss things to consider when moving a relative from out of state or into your home.

Throughout this book, charts and graphics highlight important points and offer information in new, interesting formats. Contributions by experts in dementia care are scattered throughout the book, addressing topics as diverse as driving, diagnosis, and end of life care.

As a comprehensive resource, *Moving A Relative & Other Transitions in Dementia Care* will prove invaluable to families as they navigate transitions from the beginning of their caregiving journey to the end of their relative's life.

Henry L. Paulson, MD, PhD

Henry L. Paulson, MD, PhD, is the Lucile Groff Professor of Neurology for Alzheimer's Disease and Related Disorders in the Department of Neurology at the University of Michigan. Dr. Paulson joined the U-M faculty in 2007, and he currently directs the Michigan Alzheimer's Disease Center (MADC) and co-directs the U-M Protein Folding Diseases Initiative.

INTRODUCTION

We (Laurie and Beth) set out to update our previous book, *Moving a Relative with Memory Loss: A Family Caregiver's Guide*. In the process we realized that we had much more to say about the many decisions and transitions that families face when a relative has dementia. Content from the *Moving* book has been included, expanded and updated, but now this book incorporates much more from our many years of geriatric social work and caregiver counseling.

"When my mom's Alzheimer's disease progressed to the point where she was not safe living alone, I knew there had to be someone who could help me, but who? Where? Was moving her the only choice I had? Not knowing if there were other options, added another level of stress for me. I felt completely alone and in the dark."

This is a common scenario. It can be very stressful for families who are trying to keep their relative at home when they have concerns about a relative's safety and are concerned about their ability to keep up with their relative's needs.

Frequently families do not know where to turn for help and information about programs and services that might be available. This book offers suggestions about evaluating safety and information about in-home services and adult day programs that may postpone or eliminate the need to move a relative. We've added some considerations for getting your relative to accept these services and, as in prior editions, how to make the process of moving your relative as easy as possible if and when it becomes necessary. We have also added thoughts about moving relatives across state lines.

There were other key decision points and transitions that we felt needed expertise other than ours. We invited eight experts in various areas of dementia care to contribute pieces. These include decisions about diagnosis, driving, choosing the best care, building relationships with staff, hospital and end of life care, as well as information about what happens to a person's insight when he or she has dementia. We have also added a short section to help you understand how brain changes affect decision-making and judgment in people with dementia.

Since we began working with caregivers and people with dementia in the early 1980's, the number of programs and support services for families has increased dramatically. There are more in-home care agencies, adult day programs and residential care communities, many of which have been designed specifically for individuals with memory loss. Learning how to locate and negotiate the array of services for someone with dementia can be overwhelming. The next step – getting your relative to accept help from you or others – can be challenging, especially when he or she does not recognize the need for assistance and support. This book is intended to help families who are caring for a relative with dementia and who are experiencing challenges taking care of her safely, taking care of personal needs and accepting assistance and suggestions from family and friends. It is our hope, that the information offered in this book will help you find available options and consider some steps to take to help your relative… and you.

The authors pictured in the 1990s.

ABOUT THIS BOOK

We invited eight experts in dementia care to contribute short articles. Each piece addresses a pivotal transition that builds on the contributing author's expertise.

Residential Care Homes, Assisted Living, Memory Care Communities, Nursing Homes.

In writing this book we are faced with a dilemma about what to call residential care. We have chosen not to use the term "facility" because it is a very institutional term and many places are trying to move away from institutional care. Some of the ideas we suggest may apply more to assisted living than nursing homes. However, most apply to a broad range of living situations.

For the most part, we have opted to use "residential care," "residential home" or "care home" to describe this whole range of possibilities. We recognize, however, that nursing home care may be very different from life in a private pay assisted living community or in a small board and care home. As we have indicated where appropriate, terminology and regulations differ from state to state.

A word about gender

Throughout these pages, we have mostly used "she" or "her" to refer to the person with memory loss or dementia. We know that some of your relatives are men, but we chose to use the female pronouns simply because there are many more older women than men who have dementia.

Legal authority

We have assumed throughout this book, that you or other family members have the legal authority to make decisions for your relative, including the decision whether to move your relative to a residential care setting. The terminology and laws differ slightly from state to state. If you are not clear about your legal status in this area, we suggest you talk with an attorney or direct questions to the Area Agency on Aging, or your local chapter of the Alzheimer's Association. Resources are provided throughout the book.

Case vignettes

We have included short case vignettes to illustrate how some families have managed and reacted to various situations. While these are based on real situations, we have changed the names of people we have worked with to protect their identities. We hope these case studies will help shed light on the range of situations and feelings that families experience in making the decision about what care is best for their relative, whether it be in the home, in a community based program or in a residential care setting.

GRAPHICS

We decided to use graphics and illustrations in this book - both to give difficult subjects a lighter feel but also to help differentiate between different types of information. As you look at the book, please note:

Case studies look like the one at the beginning of this introduction.

Our **expert contributors'** pages begin with an envelope image and the contributor's bio.

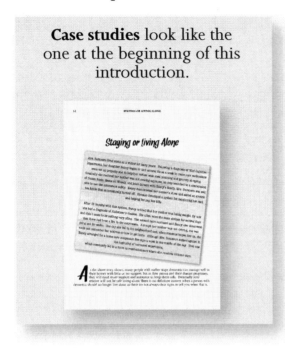

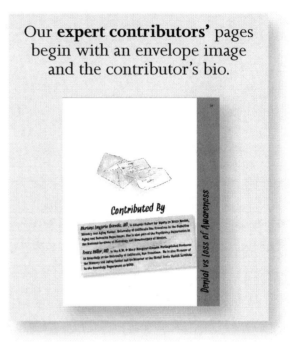

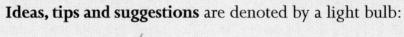

Ideas, tips and suggestions are denoted by a light bulb:

Website resources have this symbol beside them:

Please visit our website to contact us or to read dementia care blogs on a number of topics not included in this book.

www.dementiacarebooks.com

Laurie White
Beth Spencer

The Starting Point

The Starting Point

We are often asked, "What is dementia? Is dementia the same as Alzheimer's disease?"

The following brief descriptions of the most common types of dementia and their symptoms are intended to help you begin to understand each type of dementia, their similarities and their differences. In recent years, progress has been made in our understanding of how the brain works and of various types of dementia. Technology has helped to differentiate between types of dementia, but it often remains a complex and lengthy process.

Dementia is not a specific disease but rather it is an 'umbrella' term which describes a group of cognitive symptoms including memory loss, confusion, disorientation, and difficulty performing complex tasks. There are many causes of dementia: some are treatable, and some are not.

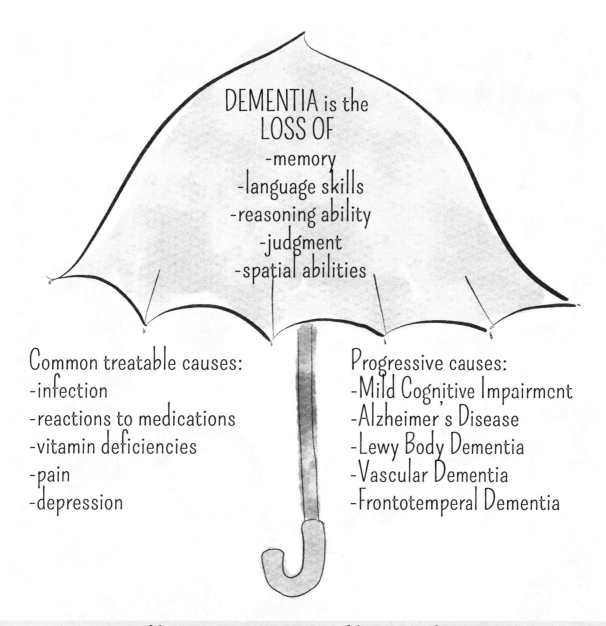

DEMENTIA is the
LOSS OF
-memory
-language skills
-reasoning ability
-judgment
-spatial abilities

Common treatable causes:
-infection
-reactions to medications
-vitamin deficiencies
-pain
-depression

Progressive causes:
-Mild Cognitive Impairment
-Alzheimer's Disease
-Lewy Body Dementia
-Vascular Dementia
-Frontotemperal Dementia

Treatable or Sometimes Reversible Types of Dementia

Conditions such as vitamin deficiencies, depression, reaction to medications, metabolic diseases or infections can affect a person's abilities to remember and to do things, can cause confusion, affect mood and behavior and cause other symptoms of dementia. When these conditions are identified and treated, the symptoms of dementia may decrease or disappear altogether. Common treatable causes of dementia are listed in the illustration on the left side of the umbrella handle. A good place to start is to talk to your relative's doctor about tests that can be performed to rule out any possible treatable cause(s) of dementia. Many of these conditions can be present along with a progressive type of dementia. It can be challenging for families and for health care professionals to sort out whether increased confusion or behavior changes are due to a urinary tract infection, for example, or are the progression of Alzheimer's disease or another type of dementia.

Progressive Types of Dementia

To the right of the umbrella handle are the most common types of dementia that are progressive, meaning they get worse over time. There are many other causes of dementia, too numerous to list. With any of these progressive neurological diseases, changes in the brain will affect a person's ability to care for herself, perform tasks, make decisions and use good judgment.

Links to on-line resources that offer more information about each of the types of dementia are listed below.

Mild Cognitive Impairment (MCI) or Mild Neurocognitive Disorder

are terms used to identify people with mild cognitive changes who are not functionally impaired enough to meet the criteria for dementia. MCI is more than just memory changes that occur as we get older, but less severe than Alzheimer's disease. Misplacing things, forgetting a recent visitor's name, slow to process what is being said can be among the first symptoms of MCI. People with MCI are usually aware of the changes in memory and compensate for their forgetfulness by writing notes and keeping a calendar of events. Other cognitive changes associated with MCI are changes in language, judgement and decision making. This level of cognitive change does not typically interfere with daily functioning. The level of memory loss with MCI can be stable for years. Some individuals do develop memory and functional impairment consistent with Alzheimer's disease or another form of dementia.

Resources for more information about MCI:

www.alz.org

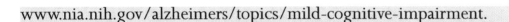
www.nia.nih.gov/alzheimers/topics/mild-cognitive-impairment.

Alzheimers' Disease

is the most common form of dementia. The Alzheimer's Association reports that 60-80% of cases of dementia are Alzheimer's disease. Memory loss is the hallmark of Alzheimer's disease. Forgetting recent events and experiences, how to perform familiar tasks such as using a computer or a programmed appliance or balancing the checkbook are commonly some of the first signs of Alzheimer's disease. The progression of Alzheimer's disease and the speed at which the symptoms occur varies from person to person, though symptoms increase over time. As the disease progresses, other changes occur: difficulty with word finding, decision making, problem solving and reasoning and using poor judgment. In the later stages, people usually develop mobility problems, become incontinent and dependent on others for care. This is often the time that families begin to explore services in and outside of the home.

For further information about Alzheimer's disease visit the Alzheimer's Association's website: www.alz.org

www.nia.nih.gov/health/what-alzheimers-disease

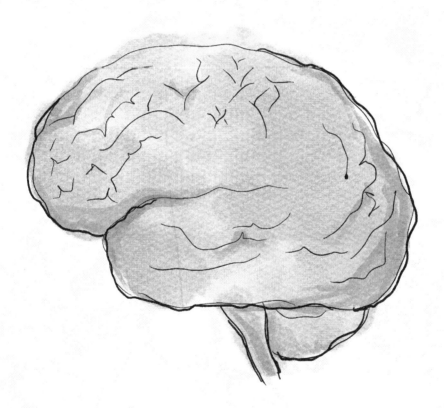

Lewy Body dementias

include both Parkinson's disease with dementia and Lewy Body disease. The order in which symptoms appear may determine the name given to the dsease, but many researchers and physicians consider these diseases to be related. More information about each is on the next page.

Lewy Body Disease (LBD)

has become the second most commonly diagnosed form of dementia in the past 20 years. Large day to day fluctuations in cognitive abilities and alertness, as well as hallucinations, are the hallmarks of LBD. Many families report that it took months or years to receive an accurate diagnose for their relative because the initial symptoms can resemble either Alzheimer's or Parkinson's disease, or on a good day the person may seem normal. Sleep disorders can precede the diagnosis. Over time, changes in behavior, mood, processing visual and auditory information, alertness and mobility occur.

The Lewy Body Dementia Association's website offers educational materials, blogs and hosts webinars for family and professional caregivers:

www.LBDA.org

www.nia.nih.gov/health/what-lewy-body-dementia

Parkinson's Disease (PD)

is also a progressive neurological disorder characterized by mobility problems, tremors, lack of facial expressions and slow gait. When a person has lived with the movement problems for at least a year, and then develops dementia, it is often called Parkinson's disease with dementia.

Information on symptom management can be found at:

www.parkinsons.org

www.nia.nih.gov/health/parkinsons-disease

Vascular Dementia

is a term that describes dementia caused by vascular disease in the brain. Vascular disease is disease of the arteries and veins and can occur anywhere in the body. Vascular dementia is difficult to diagnose because the presenting symptoms can be very similar to Alzheimer's disease. If it is determined that a person has vascular dementia and Alzheimer's disease, it may be called mixed dementia.

www.nia.nih.gov/health/vascular-contributions-cognitive-impairment-and-dementia

Mixed Dementia

is a term that is sometimes given when it is determined that a person has more than one type of dementia. Most people with mixed dementia are diagnosed and treated for symptoms that are most characteristic of one type of dementia. It is only after death and when an autopsy is performed that mixed dementia can be confirmed.

Frontotemporal Dementias (FTD)

affect the frontal lobe (forehead area) and temporal lobes (side of head). The majority of people with FTD are in the 45- 65 age group. There are several forms of FTD. The hallmarks of FTD are not memory loss, but changes in a person's personality, behavior and language. Loss of impulse control resulting in displaying socially inappropriate behavior is common. As the diseases progress, it becomes harder for the person with FTD to plan and organize.

More information about the various types of FTD can be found at:
www.theaftd.org

www.nia.nih.gov/health/what-are-frontotemporal-disorders

12

Brain Changes That Can Affect Decision Making

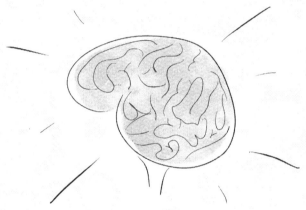

When people develop a progressive, neurological dementia such as Alzheimer's disease (AD), frontotemporal dementia (FTD) or Lewy Body Dementia (LBD), many changes occur in their brains. These changes happen gradually and affect the person's thinking and abilities related to normal functioning. As family members, we often struggle to understand what we are seeing, what our relatives can or can't do, and how much to involve them in decisions. In this section, we will discuss some of these changes and how they might relate to actions and decision-making. The type of dementia the person has will affect how and when these changes occur.

There is great variability from individual to individual. Some of us have great memories to begin with; others do not. Some of us are known for our wisdom and insight; others of us are not as strong in these areas. When people develop dementia, their previous cognitive strengths and weaknesses will come into play in addition to the brain changes caused by disease.

The case studies below discuss a few of the many cognitive changes that are part of what we call "executive function." These cognitive areas work together to allow us to get through our days, to perform routine tasks, to make good decisions and to solve problems that are familiar to us. When several of these functions are impaired, the result may be inability to think clearly, do routine tasks and make good decisions.

Memory Loss

While short term memory loss is the hallmark of Alzheimer's disease (AD), it is much less prominent in the early stages of Lewy Body Dementia (LBD). Memory loss can make decisions difficult for several reasons. The person may not remember key pieces of information. For example, a woman whose driver's license has been suspended may forget this and continue to drive illegally.

When discussing the need for her father to move in with her, Pat found that he could not remember from moment to moment that he had a brain disease affecting his ability to live alone. He would acknowledge it when Pat pointed it out, but forget it within the next few minutes.

Planning & Organizing

Sara, below, is having difficulty with planning and organizing. This shows up in many ways - in people's inability to begin or stop an action, to shift gears from one activity to another or to think through the steps involved in activities. These are some of the executive functions that are eventually impaired in all forms of dementia.

Sara has Alzheimer's disease. When she wakes up in the morning, she lies in bed and tries to figure out what she is supposed to do. Because many of her executive functions are impaired, she no longer remembers what her normal morning routine is. While she can get herself out of bed, she doesn't know what to do next. She can get herself dressed but her husband has to prompt her. She no longer remembers the right order of clothing and she has difficulty initiating each step. Although Sara can carry on a social conversation which often fools people, she doesn't always know to whom she is talking.

Judgment

It is difficult to determine exactly when judgment becomes impaired, but unfortunately many people have made very poor decisions based on impaired judgment as in the example below of George. In frontotemporal dementias (FTD) this is one of the hallmarks. While judgment will eventually be impaired in other kinds of dementia, it may not happen as early as we see in FTD. In the example below, the frontal lobes of George's brain are damaged affecting his ability to make sound decisions. The frontal lobes are where judgment, decision-making and social inhibitions are housed.

George is in the early stages of a frontotemporal dementia, which has not yet been diagnosed. He has been a very successful businessman, but lately his business partner has been concerned because George seems to be making some bad decisions. He appears to have given a large sum of the company's money to his nephew without consulting his partner, something he has never done before.

Social Appropriateness

Saying and doing thing impulsively can be symptoms of FTD. The part of the brain that controls impulse behavior is the frontal lobes which can also be affected by Lewy Body or Alzheimer's disease.

While sitting in the waiting room of her doctor's office, Elizabeth made loud, insulting comments when people were called by the nurse. Her daughter was embarrassed and shocked by this unusual behavior.

Insight vs. Denial

There is a part of our brain that gives us insight into ourselves: how we feel, what we need and what we are capable of doing. (See *Denial vs. Loss of Awareness: The Importance of Insight in Dementia*.)

Insight

After Kathy was diagnosed with Alzheimer's disease, she noticed that she was not able to drive safely on the road. She was distracted easily and found that cars were honking at her when she was slow to start at a green light or stopped way before reaching the stop sign. "I am not comfortable or safe on the road and I need to stop driving."

Denial

Gretchen's daughter was alarmed about the way her mother was driving. After driving with her several times, Linda sat down and said to Gretchen that it may be time to stop driving. Gretchen replied "I don't know what you are talking about. I have been a great driver for 55 years and I am perfectly safe on the road." Linda was not surprised at her mother's reaction because her mother used denial throughout her life when she didn't want to accept or deal with something.

Attention

People with dementia are often easily distracted by sights, sounds and activity around them. The inability to follow a conversation and concentrate on a task usually gets worse as dementia progresses.

Cynthia loved to bake cookies for her grandchildren, but she found that it took her much longer than it used to. "I have made these recipes for years. "Now I can't remember how much and what ingredients to add to the bowl even though I just read the recipe. I have to double check myself each step of the way and I often make mistakes."

Walter, a devout Christian, became restless and anxious at church. He became impatient during the sermon, often wanting to leave. His wife found that bringing a sketch pad and some colored pencils so he could draw calmed him down, but even with the drawing pad, they often had to leave the service early.

Problem Solving And Manipulating Numbers

Individuals who have been good at solving problems and thinking through situations, gradually lose this ability when they have dementia. However, families often do not recognize that this is happening. In addition, difficulty in working with numbers is often an early warning sign of Alzheimer's disease.

Helen, a Certified Public Accountant, began making mistakes when she did her family's quarterly tax returns. In the doctor's office, she had difficulty with the part of the dementia screen where one subtracts from 100 by 7's - something she could have done with ease a few years earlier. She also began to have trouble with simple reasoning: When her husband asked her to think about whether they could afford a new car or should buy a used one, she could not figure it out.

Contributed By

Mariana Longoria Ibarrola, MD, is Atlantic Fellow for Equity in Brain Health, Memory and Aging Center, University of California San Francisco in the Cognitive Aging and Dementia Department. She is also part of the Psychiatry Department at the National Institute of Neurology and Neurosurgery of Mexico.

Bruce Miller, MD, is the A.W. & Mary Margaret Clausen Distinguished Professor in Neurology at the University of California, San Francisco. He is also Director of the Memory and Aging Center and Co-Director of the Global Brain Health Institute in the Neurology Department at UCSF.

Mariana Longoria Ibarrola, MD
Bruce Miller, MD

> *People often say that this or that person has not yet found himself*
> *But the self is not something one finds; it is something one creates*
>
> *Thomas Szasz*

The concept of insight and denial

Please imagine this scenario:

A nice, kindly and well educated woman of 80 years old arrives with her daughter at the physician's office. During the interview the patient conducts herself with respect and calm, until the moment her daughter, her primary caregiver, expresses concern about the patient's behavior. The daughter reports that her mother wants to drive even after her primary care physician prohibited this. She insists on leaving for work in the early morning even though she retired 17 years ago. She insists that relatives have visited her when they haven't and refuses to take the medication as she considers herself healthy. At this point the patient begins to argue with her caregiver and doctor, insisting that she is perfectly healthy.

This is a common scenario among patients with dementia, their caregivers, and health or mental health professionals. The basis for this problem is that many patients with Alzheimer's disease and related disorders lack awareness of their deficits. They suffer from memory issues that make this issue more complex. Also they sometimes respond to the memory loss and lack of awareness with strongly held false memories (confabulations).[1] Insight can be defined as awareness of one's illness and of how the illness is affecting oneself. Conversely, loss of insight is the person's lack of awareness into one's own behaviors or actions. Loss of insight is common in Alzheimer's disease, even in the early stages, and tends to worsen as the disease progresses. [1,2] This loss of insight into one's own deficits is often baffling to caregivers who are used to having honest conversations with their loved ones about many things, including the topics in this book. It is easy to exacerbate conflicts triggered by these denials, compounding the tensions that they create. One of the most difficult aspects of this diminishing self-awareness for family members is that their loved ones once held good insight and a strongly integrated sense of self.

The term anosognosia is used to capture lack of awareness in the presence of a neurological illness. It has been reported in different neurological and psychiatric illnesses including stroke, Parkinson's Disease, traumatic brain injury, Alzheimer's disease, frontotemporal dementia, and mild cognitive impairment. Anosognosia is a direct effect of brain disease or injury, even though psychological mechanisms can contribute to this syndrome. [4,5] As our understanding of human behavior increases with advances in neuroscience, we are recognizing that how we understand ourselves and our relationships to other people and the world, is eventually impaired in diseases that cause dementia.

Individuals can have mild and fluctuating loss of insight around specific aspects of the illness like memory loss, or more severe and constant deficits associated with false beliefs and paranoia. Alterations in mood, anxiety or irritability can make diminished insight worse. Events like the flu, new medications or changes in well-established daily patterns can be enough to make a patient paranoid, accusatory and unable to realize what is happening in their world. [6]

> *A patient can abstractly understand that they have an illness, with specific symptoms but not be aware of how it is affecting them*

Coming back to our initial case, a patient can abstractly understand that they have an illness, with specific symptoms but not be aware of how it is affecting them. Forgetfulness is an important factor in loss of insight and many patients with decreased insight have a diminishing memory of their daily experiences. In many instances, forgetful patients fill in with false information what they don't remember. Yet, they maintain a self-image of the person that they used to be - a person with a fabulous memory. This mismatch is a critical factor in the conflicts that occur with caregivers who realize that the patient is offering false memories for facts.

Another symptom that sometimes happens is called the Capgras delusion. When this is present, the person believes that the family member or friend in front of them is an imposter. The relative becomes a threatening figure who is insisting that they are the patient's loved one. This is terribly upsetting to caregivers, who find that arguing does not help. The patient's reality is that they are imposters. [2,3,7]

Donald's wife had a diagnosis of Lewy Body Dementia. At a certain point in the illness, she began to accuse him of being a stranger. She would become frightened and ask him where her husband was. Sometimes she told him to get out of her house. Donald found that if he left and called her, she would recognize his voice on the phone and he could calm her down. He did not argue with her about the "stranger." He just reassured her that he would be home soon. Usually when he returned, she recognized him.

Approach to Denial of Illness

Most experienced caregivers suggest that confrontation regarding diminished insight is rarely if ever helpful. Keeping calm, non-accusatory, warm and supportive is important. Distracting patients rather than explaining why their false beliefs are wrong is the best approach. Dementia is a progressive problem and symptoms that are troublesome at one point can quickly diminish or disappear as in the example above. A systematic medical review of the patient's medical status with consideration of possible causes for the denial is helpful, but will not always turn up a cause. The cause is the disease and maintaining strength, without assigning blame is critical.

lack of insight highlights

HOW IT LOOKS...
-voluntary denial
-lying
-confusion
-avoiding being ill
-inflexibility
-irresponsibility

WHAT IT REALLY IS...
-lack of awareness
-confabulation (false memories)
-diminished insight (anosognosia)
-forgetfulness
-misjudgement

WHAT IS HAPPENING IN THE BRAIN...
-anosognosia is a direct effect of brain dysfunction
-damaged brain regions are in charge of
    -assessing, monitoring, and regulating one's knowledge
    -memory processing, risk evaluation, decision making, behavior,
    judgment, and regulation of emotional expression
-challenging behaviors reach a peak as the
disease progresses but in late stages,
they tend to disappear

WHAT TO THINK...
-keep in mind anosognosia is a
symptom of the disease
-try to evaluate all aspects of the
situation
-remember security is a priority
-use empathy and forgiveness, two
powerful tools
-find humor in little details
-it's not personal

WHAT TO DO...
-avoid confrontation
-keep calm, be warm and supportive
-use distraction as much as possible
-be creative and use different
approaches
-when reporting symptoms be
mindful of the patient's feelings
-remember caring is a long path
where you learn daily

References

[1] Henna Leich, Martin Berwig, Hermann-Josef Gertz (2010) Anosognosia in Alzheimer´s Disease: the role of impairment levels in assessment of insight across domains, Journal of the International Neuropsychological Society 16, 463-473.

[2] I.S. Marková, German E. Berrios (1992) The Meaning of Insight in Clinical Psychiatry, British Journal of Psychiatry 160, 850-860.

[3] Sergio Starkstein (2014) Anosognosia in Alzheimer´s disease: Diagnosis, frequency, mechanism and clinical correlates, Cortex 61, 64-73.

[4] Howard J. Rosen (2011) Anosognosia in neurodegenerative disease, Neurocase 17:3, 231-241.

[5] Ivana S. Marková Dr, Linda Clare, Michael Wang, Barbara Romero & Geraldine Kenny (2005) Awareness in dementia: Conceptual issues, Aging & Mental Health 9:5, 386-393.

[6] I.S. Marková, German E. Berrios (2014), The construction of anosognosia: History and implications, Cortex 61, 9-17.

[7] William Hirstein (2010) The misidentification syndromes as mindreading disorders, Cognitive Neuropsychiatry 15:1-3, 233-260.

Getting A Diagnosis

Getting A Diagnosis

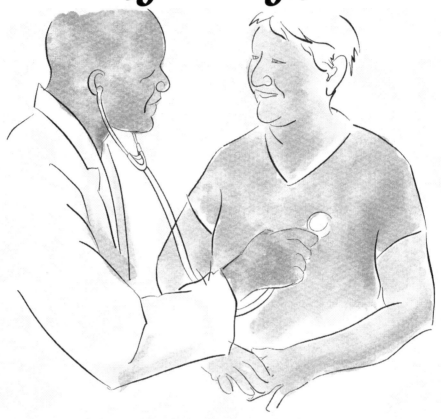

What Is Involved In Getting A Diagnosis?

Currently no definitive diagnostic clinical test exists for Alzheimer's disease, Lewy Body Dementia or most of the other progressive forms of dementia. However, a good evaluation by a knowledgeable and experienced physician can provide a diagnosis of dementia nearly all of the time. A great deal of research is in progress now with the goal of developing reliable diagnostic tests.

The diagnostic process for Mild Cognitive Impairment (MCI) or for a progressive dementia such as Alzheimer's disease or another form of dementia is similar. The goal of the process is to obtain a good description of the symptoms, understand an individual's overall health, and "rule in or out" many conditions that can cause changes in memory and thinking. A comprehensive diagnostic process includes the following:

- A good history, including symptoms and past medical and mental health conditions.

- A physical and a neurological exam.

- Laboratory tests, where blood is drawn to test for specific conditions.

- Cognitive screening or full neuropsychological testing.

- A brief screening test is often administered in the doctor's office. Examples include the Mini Mental Status Exam (MMSE) or the Montreal Cognitive Assessment (MOCA). A lengthier neuropsychological test is generally conducted and interpreted by a professionally trained neuropsychologist. In appropriate circumstances, formal neuropsychological testing may assist in providing information to help improve the accuracy of a diagnosis.

- Brain imaging, usually consisting of a cranial tomography (CT) scan or a magnetic resonance image (MRI).

- Special tests, such as a positron emission tomography (PET) scan, electroencephalogram (EEG), lumbar puncture (LP), and sleep studies, are sometimes useful to evaluate for unusual causes of dementia.

Sometimes, when the usual tests do not provide a clear diagnosis, the diagnostic process becomes a "wait and see" situation. Watching for changes in symptoms which do or don't occur over a 6 to 12 month period, for example, can give clues about what is happening in the brain.

What Kind Of Physician Can Provide A Diagnosis?

When the diagnosis is fairly straightforward, as it sometimes is with Alzheimer's disease for example, a family doctor, internist, or other primary care physician may be able to provide a reliable diagnosis. If you are not sure, ask the doctor how comfortable he or she is with the work up elements outlined earlier.

The physician may feel more comfortable referring your relative to a more specialized clinic.

Neurologists, psychiatrists and geriatricians often conduct the diagnostic process.

How Do I Find A More Specialized Clinic?

◦ Contact the Alzheimer's Association in your area:

https://www.alz.org/ or 800-272-3900

◦ National Alzheimer's Disease Centers, through the National Institute on Aging are another good resource. The link below shows a map of the centers around the country. Readers can look on the map to see if there is one located near them.

https://www.nia.nih.gov/health/alzheimers-disease-research-centers

◦ Large medical centers and health systems often have specialized clinics through their neurology departments.

What If My Relative Refuses To Go To The Doctor Or To Get A Work Up?

Here are some of the things that families have said or done to get their relatives to a doctor:

For the initial screening,

Frank told his wife that they were both getting older and needed to have everything checked out. He scheduled a geriatric assessment for himself and for his wife, although it was really his wife's memory he was concerned about.

"I told my mother

that I was concerned about her health and well-being as she got older and that I would feel better if she would get a check-up. She was reluctant, but she agreed."

"My husband knew

he had memory loss but was afraid to go to the doctor. I reminded him that lots of things can cause memory problems and that some of them are fixable."

"My father was already too confused

to reason with, but he loved food. I promised him a hot fudge Sunday after the doctor appointment."

"Our family all got together

and kind of ganged up on my mom. She gave in because so many of us insisted. We asked her who she would like to go with her and she chose me."

"My mother had not gone

to the doctor in years, and she repeatedly told me that she wasn't about to start now. I made the appointment and told her about the appointment on the way there. I said I was so worried about her that I was not sleeping or eating well. She didn't like it, but she did go in the office for me."

"I had tried several times,

and was getting more frustrated and angry at her refusal to go which only made her more resistant. I knew my mom's best friend had gone to the doctor about her memory changes, and asked her to talk to my mom. She did and my mom eventually agreed to go because her friend had."

"I called her doctor

and asked him to call her to come in for a check-up and to make the appointment right away, so she was more likely to remember."

Sometimes no matter what families do, their relative refuses to go to the doctor. If this is the case, wait and try again in a few months.

Contributed By

Nancy Barbas, MD, MSW, is Associate Professor of Neurology at Michigan Medicine, Ann Arbor, Michigan where she served as Director of the Cognitive Disorder Clinic for 12 years and continues as member of the Executive Committee and consultant to the Michigan Alzheimer's Disease Center. She takes great pleasure in teaching the next generation of physicians at the University of Michigan in courses on Doctoring and Medical Humanities.

Nancy Barbas, MD, MSW

Sharon, age 74, notices she can't remember the names of new acquaintances and even her neighbors the way she used to. Is this normal, she wonders.

A younger man, Ken, has been told by his employer that he is missing deadlines. and his productivity has slipped. He can't put his finger on why this is happening. Can he continue to work? Will he make a regrettable mistake?

At her granddaughter's birthday party, several relatives have confided that they are worried about Sally's husband who seems quieter and more withdrawn. Sally has been recognizing this for months. Maybe she should let his doctor know?

We Are All Different

For some, the decision to seek evaluation for their memory and cognitive abilities is easy. For others, this decision may represent a burden or a frightening step. Whether and when to seek evaluation for memory and cognitive difficulties is different for everyone. A first step to diagnosis is gaining knowledge about the process. What does it mean to seek diagnostic evaluation through their health care provider? What can be gained?

> Whether and when to seek evaluation for memory and cognitive difficulties is different for everyone.

People with symptoms of dementia often go undiagnosed. Researchers have observed that one to four years goes by from the time a person or their loved one notices they have changed until an evaluation takes place. What causes these delays?

- An individual experiencing the changes of dementia may not recognize or be aware of them. Because the changes that accompany dementia often occur slowly, they also may go unrecognized by family and health care providers.

- A person may be fearful of stigma or loss attached to receiving a diagnosis.

- Patients and providers may lack knowledge about diseases that cause dementia and their treatment.

- A person may face barriers to receiving care such as limited clinic or health care provider availability, high costs for care, and lack of insurance.

We now recognize the importance of addressing dementia early and there are many national guidelines, programs and policies aimed at improving screening and assessment of dementia. One of these is the Annual Wellness Evaluation program offered through Medicare to patients age 65 and older. The evaluation includes a screening assessment and tests for memory and cognitive and mood changes that could represent the onset of dementia or depression.

What is meant by "early diagnosis of dementia"? "Dementia" refers to the medical condition in which a person has experienced a change in memory or cognitive ability which interferes with their usual abilities. It is often, though not always, progressive. "Early" refers to the stage of the condition after symptoms are first noticed. Alzheimer's disease is the most common, and one of several types of dementia resulting from degeneration of cells in the central nervous system or brain. Mild Cognitive Impairment describes a condition in which a person has changes in their memory or thinking ability which do not interfere with their usual abilities. Some researchers and physicians feel this is a very mild form or precursor to dementia.

Why Diagnose Early

The primary goal of early diagnosis of dementia and Alzheimer's disease is to assist the patient, and inevitably the patient's family and caregivers, in maintaining high quality of life as they face a chronic, progressive disease. Everyone can expect a different experience depending on the individual person, their caregivers and family members, and the specific disease that is present.

A person or their family member may be aware that something about them has changed and they are often relieved when they receive a diagnosis which can serve as validation to their beliefs. Though often feared, studies have reported that there is a low occurrence of anxiety or depression that is most often brief and temporary after a person learns of their dementia diagnosis. [1]

Patients who seek evaluation early after symptoms develop can receive many benefits.

> ⁰ Their evaluation may result in identification of medical factors or diseases that may be easily treatable or even reversible. For example, changes in thinking may be the result of an undesirable medication side effect or untreated medical disorder such as thyroid disease or a severe sleep disorder.

Early evaluation may result in identification of medical factors or diseases that may be easily treatable or even reversible.

> ⁰ They may be offered medications or other treatments that serve to maintain them at the highest level possible, at a time when early intervention is most meaningful.
>
> ⁰ A person may receive knowledge that can contribute to their autonomy. They are given the opportunity to participate in advanced planning and

decision making regarding future financial, health, end of life wishes and other components of their life.

Caregivers, too, benefit from a patient's early evaluation.

> ⁰ Caregivers often experience a sense of relief when their suspicions are confirmed and a name is given to an ambiguous feeling. They may find it easier to understand the reasons behind a loved one's actions and behaviors. [2]
>
> ⁰ With a diagnosis, family may feel more comfortable taking on a caregiver role. This may allow them to experience loss and grief as well as offer the opportunity to learn coping skills and adaptive strategies.
>
> ⁰ When a diagnosis is made early in the disease course, caregivers and patients are sometimes able to build an alliance and nourish a model of joint decision making.
>
> ⁰ When early assessment and diagnosis occur, the patient, caregiver and healthcare provider can work together as a team. Working together as a team can prove to be very beneficial.

⊙ Open discussions about prognosis, safety, risks, and treatment are facilitated.

⊙ Opportunities for research participation can be offered and considered.

⊙ When patients and their families have an opportunity to learn of prognosis and support services, it is easier to cope with the neuropsychological and behavioral symptoms that commonly accompany dementia as it advances.[3]

⊙ Patients can actively participate in planning for their future with the support of the team.

When first discussing the evaluation for symptoms of dementia and receiving a dementia diagnosis, and throughout the treatment process, every patient should expect respect, privacy and confidentiality. **Early assessment and diagnosis contribute to the design of a personalized and comprehensive care plan in which the patient, caregiver and healthcare provider can undertake decision making as a team.** Overall, properly done, the undertaking of early diagnosis of dementia can benefit the patient, family and caregivers by promoting understanding, hope and reassurance.

References

[1] Gauthier S et al, Progress in Neurobiol, 10, 2013, 102-113.

[2] Derksen E et al 2005, VanVliet D et al 2011 as sited by deVugt ME and Verhey RJ, Progress in Neurobiol 1,10, 2013, 54-62.

[3] Olazaran J et al 2010 as sited by deVugt ME and Verhey RJ, Progress in Neurobiol 1,10, 2013, 54-62.

Staying or Living Alone: When Does it Become Unsafe?

Mrs. Summers lived alone as a widow for many years. Following a diagnosis of Mild Cognitive Impairment, her daughter Nancy began to visit several times a week to make sure medications were set up properly and to help her mother with meal planning and grocery shopping. Gradually she realized her mother was not cooking anymore, so they switched to a combination of frozen foods, Meals on Wheels, and joint dinners with Nancy's family. Mrs. Summers was still able to use the microwave safely. Nancy disconnected her mother's stove and added an electric tea kettle that automatically turned off. She also developed a system for monitoring her mail and helping her pay her bills.

After 18 months with this system, Nancy noticed that her mother was losing weight. By now she had a diagnosis of Alzheimer's disease. She often wore the same clothes for several days and didn't seem to be bathing very often. She seemed more confused and Nancy also discovered that there had been a fire in the microwave. Although her mother was not driving, she was going out for walks. One day she fell in the neighborhood and, when someone helped her up, she could not remember her address or how to get home. Although Mrs. Summers argued against it, Nancy arranged for a home care companion five days a week in the middle of the day. That was the beginning of increased supervision, which eventually led to a move to residential care where she received 24-hour care.

As the above story shows, many people with earlier stage dementia can manage well in their homes with little or no support, but as time passes and their disease progresses, they will need more support and assistance to keep them safe. Eventually your relative will not be safe living alone. There is no definitive answer when a person with dementia should no longer live alone as there are not always clear signs to tell you when that is.

As we mentioned in the Introduction, judgment and the ability to make informed decisions are affected when a person has dementia. However, these cognitive changes occur at different rates for different people. The need for increased supervision is usually a gradual process as the case study above illustrated. Every person with dementia and every set of family circumstances are unique. For example, the progression of the disease, the responses of the person to the disease, and where the person lives are factors that can impact safety.

What Should You Be Watching For?

The key to addressing these challenging issues is to continually assess safety risks. Consider the following as you make decisions about the safety of your relative.

Responding To Emergencies

Would your relative know what to do in an emergency, for example, if there were a fire in the house? This is an important question to ask. However, even if the person can answer the question correctly, it does not always mean she can actually do what's needed. It's important to ask her to demonstrate calling 911, leaving the house and going to the neighbor's, using the fire extinguisher, etc. If she is not able to respond appropriately in an emergency, how much risk are you as a family willing to tolerate?

Print a list of important phone numbers near every phone or in key locations such as on the refrigerator or a desk. Make sure the font is large enough for your relative to easily read.

Consider installing a phone with important numbers programmed in and photos or large words on the buttons to identify family, friends or neighbors who can help in an emergency. This can help people with cognitive problems use the phone independently for a longer period of time.

Managing Medications

As memory and judgment gradually worsen, taking medications accurately can become difficult and eventually impossible for people with dementia.

Use a pill box with AM & PM compartments to help your relative know what pills to take morning and night.

Ask her doctor if her medications can be simplified. Can some be eliminated? Or changed to once a day? If swallowing pills becomes difficult, are any of the medications available in a different form – a patch or a liquid may be easier.

There are now many automated medication dispensers available that dispense the pills and alert a person to take medications. If medications are not taken some services offer to call and remind the person to take her medications.   Some of these work for a while for people with mild dementia.

Set up medications together. This gives your relative the opportunity to be involved and give you the chance to see how your relative is doing setting up her medications.

If medications are becoming a battleground, try to give her as much control as possible. "Would you like your medicine now or after breakfast?" Keep in mind that some medications need to be taken with food, others before or after a meal.

Handling Alcohol

It is imperative to monitor alcohol. People with memory loss may not be able to accurately monitor how much they drink. Alcohol can also increase the risk of falling. On the other hand, a cocktail or glass of wine with dinner may be a longstanding habit that brings pleasure to your relative.

Ask your relative's physician about the appropriate amount of alcohol that is safe for your relative to drink. Try non-alcoholic beer and wine or watering down other alcoholic drinks.

Misusing Household Toxins

Pay attention to household cleaners that could be used inappropriately. Mr. Carter washed his hair with mouthwash one day. To his daughter this was a red flag that he no longer understood what the various bottles around the house were.

If you see your relative becoming mixed up about bottles, cleansers, etc., sort them out. Lock up anything toxic, e.g., paint thinner, bleach, counter top cleansers, some dishwashing soaps. Remove any bottles that are not needed or not being used.

Smoking

Does your relative smoke? If so, does she leave
burning cigarettes unattended? This can occur when
someone has memory loss or becomes confused.
If the person has a progressive dementia such as
Alzheimer's disease, unsupervised smoking can become
a dangerous problem. Working on ways to decrease or
end the smoking habit will become important. It's not
uncommon for people to forget about smoking as their
dementia progresses.

At some point, locking up matches and
lighters may become necessary. Allow your
relative to smoke only when someone
is present to make sure cigarettes are
extinguished properly.

Nicotine gum or patches can sometimes
help people stop craving cigarettes.

Leaving The Stove On

This can become dangerous when someone
with dementia forgets to turn off the stove and
burns tea kettles or pans. However, many of us
do this occasionally, so it should be interpreted
cautiously.

There are fairly straightforward ways to handle this: using
electric tea kettles with automatic shut-off, disabling the stove
by removing knobs or tripping the circuit breaker, or having
an electrician install automatic shut off timers on the stove and
oven. Many people can safely handle a simple microwave for a
period of time when stoves have become dangerous.

Unsafe Room Or Water Temperatures

As we age and our skin becomes thinner, older adults often feel colder than we do and try to warm up the house by turning the heat up too high or turning the air off in hot weather. This can put a person at risk for dehydration especially if she is not drinking enough liquids.

Programming the thermostat – day and night - to a temperature that is comfortable for your relative may prevent her from wanting to adjust the temperature too high. Making the thermostat inaccessible by encasing it in a locked plastic case can make it impossible to change the temperature.

Setting the water heater to 120 degrees is safer on a person's fragile skin and can prevent burns.

Getting Lost

Does your relative leave the house alone for walks? The National Alzheimer's Association estimates that about 60% of people with Alzheimer's disease will "wander" at some point in the illness (meaning that they may get lost, even in familiar places). If your relative is going out alone, it would be good to consider safeguards such as those below.

Some individuals are afraid to leave the house and may never be at risk of getting lost. If your relative talks a lot about going home or leaving, she may be at risk for getting lost even if she has not walked out to date.

The Alzheimer's Association and MedicAlert co-sponsor the Safe Return program.
http://www.alz.org/care/ dementia-medic-alert- safe-return.asp
Safe Return is a 24-hour emergency response system that operates nationwide.

Project Lifesaver is an international GPS based tracking system that operates in many geographic areas.
http://www.projectlifesaver.org

Leaving The House At Night

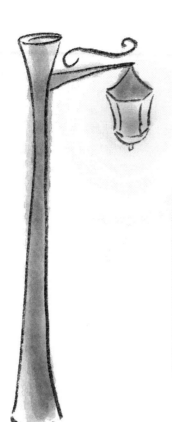

Some people in the later stages of dementia get days and nights mixed up and may get up and dressed in the middle of the night. If this is becoming a problem or if your relative has ever left the house in the middle of the night, it is important to think about supervision at night. If she is alone and has left the house during the night, she may not be safe alone at night.

If there are other people in the house, try securing the doors in some way: install an alarm system or a lock high on the door. Simple door securing devices designed for children are another option. These are available on-line and in retail stores.

Opening The Door To Strangers

What does your relative do if someone rings the doorbell? Does she open the door to strangers? People with dementia gradually lose the ability to make good decisions and judgments about what is safe and what is not safe. This can become very dangerous if she is likely to answer the door and invite a stranger in or give the person money.

A sign on the front of the house that says "No solicitations" may decrease the number of sales people knocking on the door. For some people, a large sign on the inside of the door that says "Do not open the door to anyone," solves this problem for a while.

Giving Money Away

Mail, phone, and computer solicitations make life increasingly dangerous for individuals with compromised judgment. Individuals with dementia are at high risk for financial exploitation from strangers or relatives. Some individuals with dementia make donations, either giving small amounts repeatedly or giving large amounts. Repeated credit card purchases can lead to financial difficulties. Others become addicted to internet gambling.

Phones can be changed to unlisted numbers although solicitation calls may still get through. Sometimes just turning the ringer off on the phone is enough to keep the person from answering the phone. This can be a problem, however, if family members cannot get through to their relative or if the person is waiting for a call.

Leaving a small amount in a checking account for the person to use can help her feel in control of her money. Sometimes it becomes necessary to limit access to money if a person has withdrawn more cash that can be accounted for or she can afford.

If mail is an issue, one approach is to forward mail to another address or get a PO box and have someone in the family monitor it.

Computers may be more difficult to monitor if your relative is still able to use one. Some families have limited internet access or installed child safety programs on their computers. Others monitor the computer history daily to make sure that their relative is accessing safe sites and not gambling or giving away money.

Falling Repeatedly

If your relative is falling often when she is alone, safety becomes a serious issue. In the early stages of dementia, the person may be able to use a cell phone or a lifeline system to call for help, but as the disease progresses it is likely that she will not be able to remember how to use such devices.

Check your relative's shoes for stability, comfort and non-slip soles.

Make sure that tripping hazards have been removed throughout the house: clear pathways of clutter; remove area rugs that could be a tripping hazard; increase lighting to help your relative see and negotiate pathways and hallways.

Make sure all stairways have good, solid hand railings.

Contact an occupational therapist or geriatric care manager who can help to do a home safety evaluation.

aginglifecare.org

Attempting Former Hobbies Or Chores

Some activities – hunting, woodworking, cooking, sewing, mowing the lawn, for example – may involve appliances or devices that are potentially very dangerous. Closely monitoring the person's ability to handle equipment safely becomes very important. At the same time, we want the person with dementia to be able to continue to enjoy hobbies as long as possible as this is part of what makes life meaningful.

Sometimes it becomes important to remove tools or appliances from the person's home, or to keep them under lock and key.

Some families find ways to work on hobbies together for a period of time. Jane began doing woodworking projects with her father since he no longer seemed to be safely able to operate his power equipment.

Guns and ammunition should be locked up. Because we know that a person's judgment is impaired with dementia, guns become a real hazard. With supervision, gun enthusiasts may still be able to use them safely for a period of time, but the risks will increase as dementia progresses.

Calling Frequently

If your relative calls family members or friends repeatedly, this is often a sign that she is feeling anxious and is looking for reassurance. This may be a point at which you need to think about hiring increased supervision or a companion. It is not surprising when people with memory loss feel anxious as they often forget important pieces of information to help them understand what they are supposed to be doing. That kind of anxiety may lead to safety risks such as leaving the house or inviting strangers in because they are looking for reassurance, security, or companionship.

Document how often and the times of day your relative calls. This can help you identify when your relative is feeling anxious. Hiring a companion or scheduling family visits during this time can help some people feel safer, less afraid and less confused.

How Do You Get Your Relative To Accept Help?

Respite care is a term for giving caregivers a break. This can happen in many different ways: hiring a home care worker, having family members rotate time with their relative, taking advantage of adult day programs or temporary stays in a residential setting.

While respite care is extremely important for safety and for dealing with caregiver burnout, at the same time it can be stressful to think about how to introduce new people, routines and places to your relative.

What If She Refuses?

It is not uncommon for people with dementia to refuse help of any kind, which can be hard for care partners to understand. It can help to know some common and possible reasons for not accepting help. These include:

"She's just stubborn."

We've heard lots of families make this statement about their relatives. Usually what it means is that the person with dementia is used to being in control of her own life and is still trying to be independent.

"I can take care of myself."

This is not necessarily denial. Often it has to do with changes in the brain that result in the person not understanding things accurately, such as how much assistance she needs.

"I don't need any help."

Most of us are proud of being independent, which is an important value in mainstream American culture. When people develop disabilities such as cognitive changes, they may feel humiliated. Admitting that one needs help can be a very hard thing to accept for both the person with dementia and their care partners.

"When somebody helps me, I feel useless."

Accepting help can feel like accepting the fact that one has become useless or worthless. This leads to feelings of shame and can make people very resistant to accepting help.

"I'm saving my money for a rainy day."

For older people who have spent their whole lives saving money and being thrifty, the idea of spending money on help, and especially when they think they don't need help, may be very difficult to accept. In addition, for some, the idea of a sliding scale or "charity care" makes them feel uncomfortable.

"I don't want strangers in my home or knowing my business."

"I don't trust anyone to come in my home."

Many people – both families and individuals with dementia – have a strong desire for privacy. Inviting strangers into one's home is a big step. Sometimes day programs are a better solution for that reason.

Sometimes it is the family that doesn't want help. Even though you may need it, you may at times drag your feet or find excuses.

Examine your own feelings about getting help. As family members we may have some of the same feelings and hesitations as our relatives with memory loss. Make sure you are not the one getting in the way of accepting help.

Accepting help is a big step and often a hard one. Sometimes it can be helpful to discuss this with a professional, someone who can help you sort out your emotional issues and advise you on how to proceed.

Sometimes care partners become burned out without even realizing it. It may be helpful to look at the Caregiver Responsibility Chart on the next page and think about all of the tasks you are performing, in addition to the rest of your life tasks.

Caregiver Responsibility Chart

This exercise may help you see the responsibilities that you have for your relative.
Draw a line from the caregiver (you) to the tasks that you are providing. There are
empty spaces where you can add tasks that don't show up here.

RECREATIONAL
ACTIVITIES

_____
FILL IN THE BLANK

_____
FILL IN THE BLANK

DECISION
MAKING

OTHER FAMILY
RESPONSIBILITIES

TRANSPORTATION

MEDICAL CARE

HOUSE & YARD

COMPANIONSHIP

LEGAL AFFAIRS

PROBLEM SOLVING

PERSONAL CARE

MEDICATION
MANAGEMENT

ADVOCATE

MEDICAL
APPOINTMENTS

FINANCIAL
MANAGEMENT

MEALS

SHOPPING

_____
FILL IN THE BLANK

_____
FILL IN THE BLANK

WORK
RESPONSIBILITIES

Are you surprised how much you are doing for your relative?

How do you feel seeing how many and the type of tasks you are doing?

Are some tasks more stressful than others?

Who might share these tasks with you?

Is there someone you can assign some tasks to?

What tasks can you continue to do?

Other family members

Sometimes it is other family members, who may not be as involved in the care as you are, who are resisting help.

If you are making decisions together or if money is involved you may want to bring an outside person in to help with a family meeting where you discuss some of the issues related to accepting and paying for help. This could be a friend, minister/rabbi/imam, a social worker or psychologist, a medical person, or a geriatric care manager.

www.aginglifecare.org

Bringing Help into the Home

Many families gradually bring people into the home part time as companions or housekeepers. Sometimes families may arrange for the person to spend nights at a relative's house. Families with a large support network sometimes take turns spending a few hours with their relative on a daily basis. When the person is safe for short periods of time alone, but not for 24 hours a day, seven days a week, most often a combination of approaches is tried: home care, adult day programs, regularly scheduled time with relatives.

Bringing help into the home for the first time can be very troubling to the person with dementia. She may feel insulted, or humiliated or angry or a combination of these feelings. Finding ways to make the process as easy as possible is important. Some things to consider:

Is there a familiar person who could step in to help? For example, many people have asked a neighbor, housekeeper or gardener to become a part time companion. This can happen gradually and subtly and your relative may not notice the change in role. Other families have sometimes been able to recruit and pay a neighbor or friend to be a part time companion. The person with dementia may not know they are being paid. Some families say something like, "I know you sometimes get nervous being alone for a long time. Isn't it nice that Alan wants to come spend a couple of hours with you while I am away?"

Can it be presented as help for you rather than your relative? In fact, bringing someone into the home IS help for you. It is giving you some peace of mind and may be relieving you of some of your responsibilities.

Mary's mom, Karen, lived with her and her husband. For many months Karen was fine staying alone while Mary was at work. However, Mary began to get anxious phone calls from her mother and sometimes when she got home her mother would say, "Where have you been? I've been so worried!" Mary took this as a sign that Karen needed someone with her. She decided to hire a home care agency a few hours a day, but told her mother that it was primarily to help her. She said, "Amanda will be coming in a few hours while I'm at work. She'll be helping me with laundry, cleaning, shopping and cooking, but she's available to hang out with you if you want company. You don't have to interact with her though if you don't want to. She's coming to help me." Initially Mary made sure she was home while Amanda came and made sure that Amanda understood the plan. Karen accepted help on these terms and eventually enjoyed doing things with Amanda. After several months she also allowed Amanda to help her with bathing.

Assessing your needs

Before you start searching for help, it is important to think about what you and you relative need. After you determine your needs, then you can search for the agency or worker who can provide the service you need.

- **Do** you just need someone to keep your relative company or do activities with her?

- **Do** you need someone to take your relative out for lunch, shopping, visit a park or a friend?

- **Do** you need help with household chores as Mary did in the story above?

- **Will** the person have to help your relative with personal care such as going to the bathroom, dressing or bathing?

- **Are** there medications involved? (State regulations about administering medications vary, but in some states home care aides cannot handle medications.)

Understanding home care costs

Medicare is a federal health insurance plan that "cares" for people 65 and over. The type of help that is typically needed by people with dementia (companionship, help with personal care, transportation or medications) is almost never covered by Medicare. Medicaid (or Medi-Cal in California) is a federal-state health insurance that "aids" low income people. The majority of home care for people with dementia is paid for out-of-pocket by families.

Exceptions to this could include:

- Some low-income individuals who qualify for Medicaid (Medi-Cal in California).

- Veterans who meet specific guidelines.
  benefits.va.gov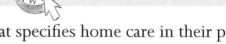

- Individuals with long term care insurance that specifies home care in their policy or under certain circumstances.

Medicare essentially only pays for home care when it is short term and involves rehabilitation of some kind. Medical home care, sometimes known as skilled care in the home, covers services such as physical therapy, injections, wound care, etc. These services need to be ordered by a doctor and are often covered by Medicare.

Finding home care

Over the past 20 years, the number of home care agencies for older adults has increased dramatically.

- Most are for-profit; some are non-profit.

- Some provide companions only. Others have trained certified nursing assistants (CNAs), nurses, physical therapists, etc.

- Some carefully screen, bond and train their staff; others do not.

- Some specialize in dementia care; others do not.

- Costs also vary but home care can be expensive.

To obtain lists of agencies in your area, contact your Area Agency on Aging (AAA). Staff at the AAA can also help you understand the different services and types of agencies in your area. You can find your AAA through the website below.
www.eldercare.acl.gov/Eldercare.NET/Public/Index.aspx

Using agencies versus private home care workers

Some families choose to use privately hired companions or home care workers instead of going through a home care agency. There are tradeoffs to doing this. An excellent tip sheet on assessing your needs and the pros and cons of each choice is available from Family Caregiver Alliance:
www.caregiver.org/hiring-home-help.

Adult Day Programs or Services (ADS).

ADS can be a helpful respite alternative. For some families, adult day programs are very helpful while they are working, doing other tasks or just resting. Not every community has such programs but many do. For the person with dementia, a good day program will provide socialization, nutritious food and well-trained staff who offer interesting, stimulating activities.

Adult day services (ADS) vary greatly. National Adult Day Services Association website:
nadsa.org

There are two common types of ADS: social day programs and health day programs. Social programs offer supervision, meals and snacks, activities and companionship. Health day programs (which include PACE) usually provide all of the above as well as rehabilitation, some medical services and may include bathing and personal care assistance.

Some ADS are expensive; others have sliding scales. They can range in cost from $25-$100+/day depending on location, services offered, number of hours attended.

ADS vary in size and format. Some social programs are small, informal, have limited hours and may be in a church or temple recreation spaces. Other programs may have 60 or more daily participants and own their own buildings. Some programs are dementia-specific; others include clients with various cognitive and physical disabilities.
As with home care, training of staff varies greatly.

PACE – Program for All Inclusive Elderly

In some communities there are PACE programs which are targeted to low income, frail older adults. These programs include medical care, adult day programs, and home care and are intended to help older people remain in their own homes as long as possible.

Finding Adult Day Services (ADS) or PACE

To find out if your community has adult day programs or PACE, contact your Area Agency on Aging, or the Alzheimer's Association.
It is important to visit and/or ask other caregivers for recommendations.

http://www.eldercare.acl.gov/Eldercare.NET/Public/Index.aspx
or
http://www.npaonline.org/pace-you/find-pace-program-your-neighborhood
or
www.alz.org

Benefits of Adult Day Services

Research has shown that there are benefits for both care partners and their relatives with attendance at day programs. For the care partners, adult day or PACE programs offer time to do other things and to be relieved of hands-on caregiving responsibilities for a few hours. Some ADS provide support groups and/or caregiver counseling as well. For the person with dementia, attendance at adult day programs can lead to decreased depression and increased socialization. Exercise and opportunities for creative expression are often provided. Some studies have found that participants in ADS adjust to assisted living or nursing home environments better than those who have not had the group experience.

Helping Your Relative Accept an Adult Day Program

It is not unusual for people with dementia to resist going to an ADS. For your relative, this may be a very scary proposition – it's unknown, there may be fears about making mistakes and fears of "being dumped in this strange place."

A number of suggestions are below:

Think about what you call the program. Does it have a name that you can use, that does not indicate it's an ADS? Some programs have names such as Gold Club or Elm Street Seniors, specifically chosen to be inviting.

Think about how you describe it. An ADS director recommended to families that they talk about it as a program for retired people. How you describe it will depend on what you think will be most non-threatening or interesting for your relative. Ask the director, social worker or intake person for help in how to present it to your relative. They typically have a lot of experience with this and have good ideas.

Take her for a visit first and choose a time with an activity that will appeal to her. Again, ask for some help with this – perhaps going for lunch together, or attending a music program would appeal to your relative.

Recognize that your relative may not be able to picture or remember it even though she's been there. Some ADS participants seem to enjoy it very much, but resist going every time.

If your relative is anxious, ask to stay with her for part of the time and/or to start with a shorter day. If you have the flexibility to do this gradually, she may have an easier adjustment.

Mr. Oaks had a terrible time every morning convincing his wife to go to the day program. The director explained that his wife probably could not remember it without some cues. She suggested he make a small photo album with pictures of the building, the front door, Mrs. Oaks' favorite staff members, and anything else that might cue her. Every day Mr. and Mrs. Oaks looked at it together in the car and it helped her understand where she was going. She was much happier about going once she had her photo book.

Recognize that your relative may not be able to picture or remember it even though she's been there. Some ADS participants seem to enjoy it very much, but resist going every time.

Reassure your relative that you will be back at a specific time. Sometimes people are afraid they are being left forever. If your relative is anxious about being there, write a note saying, "I will pick you up after your afternoon snack." Or ask staff to reassure your relative about when you will be back: It often is better to relate your pick-up time to an activity rather than a specific time. "Your daughter will be here after music."

Know that day programs are not a good fit for everyone. It's important to give it a good try over several weeks, but sometimes it just does not work. Common reasons are:

  ○ The person needs more help than the program can offer.

  ○ She may never have been a group person or a "joiner." While sometimes these people adjust very well, other times they don't.

  ○ Her anxiety or behaviors are too challenging for the program to handle.

  ○ The activities offered are not of interest to her or do not match her abilities.

Keep in mind that your relative may not accurately describe her day. During the adjustment phase, it is not unusual for a new client to report, "We didn't do anything much today. It was boring." Or, "I don't have much in common with the people there." These statements may or may not be true. Sometimes, a person may not remember what she did or the people she spent the day with. Talk to the staff about what you relative is saying and how she is adjusting to the program.

Contributed By

Ruth Gay, MS, has worked for the Alzheimer's Association for 21 years. She is currently the Chief Public Policy Officer for the Alzheimer's Association of Northern California and Northern Nevada. As an expert on the issues of policy gaps and service delivery for people with Alzheimer's disease and other dementias, Ruth directs the Federal Policy and Advocacy efforts as well as State Policy Strategic Planning for Northern California and Nevada.

Driving and Dementia

Ruth Gay, MS

Charles, a person with early stage Alzheimer's disease who was committed to his own independence, so aptly stated: "Driving provides independence from others. It is the freedom to go where you please, when you please. However, if you have been diagnosed with Alzheimer's disease or a related dementia, at some point you should stop driving."

The decision about when or if someone should stop driving

is often viewed as a tremendous loss – that of self-worth, independence and possibly a step toward serious isolation. People with Alzheimer's or dementia often experience this loss as a major impact on their independence.

What exists to replace driving?

Are there options that a community offers which are viable for someone who may not be able to drive as much, or ever again? Preparing a plan with the impacted individual can be very beneficial. A plan, which allows them a way to transition from driving to not driving is a process with several intermediate steps that can help in easing from being a driver to being a passenger. If there is strong family support, a trusted medical friend or other health professional, or a circle of friends who can participate and support this process, it can be valuable and perhaps key to a successful transition.

It is important to note that the diagnosis of Alzheimer's or dementia is not, by itself, an indicator that someone cannot drive. Taking the keys away largely depends on when the person is diagnosed and how their cognitive abilities are affected. The decision to stop driving should be made when someone is still able to participate, and before the individual is clearly a danger to themselves or others in their driving ability. Impaired decision making, reaction time, judgment, peripheral vision, disorientation, spatial skills and difficulty reasoning can be contributors to poor driving, even when the person still has the motor skills to manage the actual work of driving. The issue of driving should be a key topic for families and the individual to discuss, providing options and developing a plan.

Developing a Plan

The Alzheimer's Association has a driving resource center that offers an array of tools and information on Driving Safety. Topics include "Having the Conversation"; "Planning Ahead"; "Signs of Unsafe Driving" and "Resources". These can be a valuable first step as families or the individual decide how they should proceed once an individual has been identified as having dementia of any kind. The safety of an individual and the community is critical and family members who are concerned about someone's driving should take action, beginning with having a conversation with their loved one in a caring and supportive setting.

www.alz.org/care/alzheimers-dementia-and-driving.asp

The Hartford offers a wonderful document that lays out "Warning Signs for a Driver with Dementia" along with commitment forms with a signed agreement template that families can put together and honor when a person's skills begin to erode. This resource is free and has an array of tools and techniques to help with this difficult and increasingly common issue.

hartfordauto.thehartford.com/UI/Downloads/Crossroads.pdf

A plan should include:

○ **When or under what circumstances the person will stop driving.** A person with dementia, may not recognize signs that she is an unsafe driver.

> With her doctor's permission Karen continued to drive after her diagnosis of Alzheimer's disease. She drove to places nearby: church, the grocery store and to do other errands. After a few months, she began to feel uncomfortable driving: keeping up with traffic, negotiating detours and becoming lost scared her. She realized she had to give up the keys to keep herself and others safe on the road.

○ **Insight from significant others** who notice driving errors or close encounters. These observations should be included as an agreed upon trigger to reduce or eliminate driving.

○ **Consideration and discussion of how the person will get essential needs met.** For example, how will grocery shopping, medical appointments, and other critical engagements that allow a person to remain active in their spiritual pursuits, hobbies, clubs or other social activities be maintained?

○ **Medical advice.** A trusted physician or other health professional can be part of the discussion and recommend when it's time to no longer drive. In some states a doctor is required to report his patient to the DMV when someone should no longer drive. States have different regulations about driving. It's important to learn what they are in your state.

What is available to replace driving?

ᵒ A driver. This can provide both an outlet and a companion for the individual. Introducing new people who can help ease them from isolation and get them around can be helpful and allow the individual to remain active in their community with a sense of autonomy. The driver could be a friend, neighbor or a hired companion who is helping the person with other tasks such as housekeeping, shopping, etc. Private drivers are also available in some areas.

ᵒ Public transportation, when available can be helpful, if the individual has some history with using such transportation. When someone has cognitive impairment, and has never been a user of these services, it can be daunting and possibly confusing for them to manage this effectively.

ᵒ Specialized transportation. Most states do offer specialized transportation for people with disabilities, for which the individual may meet the criteria. When available, this may be an option, if it can be tailored to the needs of the individual.

When the person is upset or insistent on driving

ᵒ Some States offer driving programs to identify seniors at risk and to help them stay up to date on driving. These also serve as a tool to gain professional perspective on one's driving skills and can take the decision out of a family's hands and offer suggestions from an outside and perhaps more trusted resource.

Eleanor's family thought she should stop driving, but she insisted that she was okay driving. Even though they pointed out near mishaps when they rode with her, she denied she wasn't a safe driver. Eventually they hired a private driving tutor to evaluate her driving. The tutor approved of her driving the first time he took her out on the road. Six months later, he recommended that she stop driving. Eleanor took his advice and stopped but complained constantly to family about "losing her independence."

ᵒ Remove the car from sight. Some families consider removing the car once the person needs to stop driving because just seeing it parked can be a reminder of the loss, causing their relative to become upset. Others may forget they can't drive and will attempt to drive when it is not wise or safe.

° **Sell the car.** Sometimes families have success in offering to "sell the car" to a needy grandchild going off to college. Or another positive gesture, such as donating the car, can help ease the loss of ownership. Finding creative solutions can help ease the strain of this type of event.

° **Report concerns**. As a last resort, a family member or other individual can report their concerns about someone's driving to authorities anonymously. Again, the ability to do this and the rules vary from state to state.

° **Consider disabling the car** when an individual is insistent on driving despite advice or requirement not to do so.

> *Keep in mind that a person with memory loss may talk about losing the freedom to drive for weeks or months. The best strategy is to listen and acknowledge how hard this is. Despite your best efforts to reassure her that you will do everything to get her places, she may say, "Yes, but it is not the same." And as we know, indeed it isn't.*

Making The Decision To Move

Why Moving Is Hard

It's hard - don't let anyone tell you it's not. The moving decision may be one of the most difficult decisions you make in your life.

When James could no longer give his wife Helen the care that she needed without compromising his own health, he knew he had to begin to explore places where his wife would receive the best care possible. He began to think about where she might move, how he would tell her and then how best to move her. He knew that she did not want to leave their home, but at the same time, she didn't understand how much care she needed. James' son wanted his mother to stay home, but he was not available to help James provide the care. "My head knew this was the right thing to do. My heart did not. I wanted to please everyone, but I soon realized that was not possible. Moving my wife was the hardest decision I have ever had to make."

Many care partners may feel like James – saddened by the changes that dementia causes and at the same time feeling overwhelmed by the care that is needed. At this point, caregivers often begin to ask themselves, "Can I continue to care for my relative and keep her safe?" The answer to this question is not a simple one and varies from family to family.

When a family is at the point of talking about moving a parent or a partner, there are many feelings and questions that surface that can be confusing and difficult. Is it the right thing to do? Is it the right time? The right place?

Common Reactions to and Concerns about Making the Moving Decision

○ **You made promises to parents, spouses or partners.** Some spouses feel they are violating their marriage vows by moving their partner to residential care. Adult children may feel that it is "my turn to care for mom since she cared for me."

> Remind yourself that you have done the best you could in keeping promises and providing the best care possible. Sometimes we made promises that we cannot keep - when we didn't know what the future had in store. Diseases such as Alzheimer's disease or strokes are among the things that no one can predict or wants to think about.

○ **Feeling you are betraying your relative.** Some caregivers feel they are deceiving their relative when they are not able to include them in the moving decision.

> Know that most people with memory problems do not initiate a move or move voluntarily. Some people in the early stages of memory loss recognize their need for more assistance with personal care and activities and move voluntarily, but this is not usually the case. As Alzheimer's disease and other forms of dementia progress, their insight into their own needs and behavior becomes more impaired. This is a common result of brain damage caused by Alzheimer's disease, small strokes or similar illnesses. When this happens, the decision to move a relative with memory loss commonly rests on the family.
> (See *Brain Changes that Affect Decision-Making*.)

○ **Fear that your relative may be angry at you, feel sad, or be more confused after the move.**

Keep in mind that most people forgive their relatives for the moving decision. It is not uncommon for a new resident to be angry or agitated during the initial days after a move, but these feelings usually decrease as the new resident becomes adjusted to living in a new place.

Remind yourself that your relative may not remember why she had to move, even if you talked to her about it and involved her in the process.

Talk to staff and other family members about how new residents and families have coped during the adjustment period, often a period of several weeks to several months. When these feelings are expressed, it can be difficult to know how to respond or what to do. Members of caregiver support groups often talk about how they and their relative adjusted during the initial weeks and months. Hearing how others coped can be very helpful.

○ **Worry that the move will cause a faster decline.** We have found this not to be true in many cases. To a large extent this depends on your relative's medical condition, stage of dementia, and what type of place your relative is moving to. Research about this issue is inconsistent, but it is true that people who are in very poor health and move directly from home to a nursing home seem to have higher mortality rates. This does not appear to be true of people who move into assisted living when they are healthier.

It is true that it takes time for a person with dementia to adjust to her new surroundings, schedule, and to get to know other residents and staff. This may result in increased confusion for a while. Sometimes what precipitated the move was a decline and that decline may continue after the move. That does not mean that the move caused your relative to get worse.

Remember that, for all of us, adjusting to living in a new place with new people and a new routine takes time. Most new residents do adjust but it can take longer than you expect. Some new residents adjust quicker than others.

If your relative does not adjust well, ask the manager if you can talk to her. Is there something that might help her adjust, such as introducing her to a resident with a similar background and interests, involving her in activities that she might enjoy, making morning and night routines more similar to what she did at home.

○ **Moving symbolizes decline.** For many family members, the move to residential care is a very powerful symbol that the disease is progressing and the person is changing. Many families feel their relative is getting worse because they have not tried hard enough. This is rarely the case. It is difficult to accept that common forms of dementia worsen over time, despite our best efforts. This can be emotionally difficult to accept. Often family caregivers report feelings of grief - sadness, anger, denial — when their relative's abilities and needs change. During these emotional times, care partners can feel confused about what to do.

> Consider talking to a therapist or a grief counselor who is experienced in caregiving issues, and who can confirm that your feelings are common and normal.

○ **Criticism from family or friends.** Sometimes those around us reinforce our feelings of guilt and pain with insensitive comments, or with their own beliefs. It is common for caregivers to be more sensitive to others' comments when they are struggling with all the feelings associated with the idea of moving a relative: guilt, ambivalence, confusion, anger, etc.

> Try to keep in mind that friends and family members who have not "walked in your shoes" may not completely understand your situation.

> Think about whose counsel you trust and need. Try to ignore other, unsolicited advice and comments.

○ **Money.** Being concerned about finances is understandable. Residential care for people with memory loss is expensive. Not knowing if your relative will outlive her money or if the money will outlive her is very stressful. It is impossible to predict how long a person with dementia will live.

Care partners often ask themselves "Should I move her now knowing that we may run out of money or do we wait and save her money for her future care?" This is a difficult question to answer. Some families decide that moving their relative sooner may give her opportunities that she does not have now - being with others, and doing enjoyable and social activities. Other families may wait longer, saving the money they have reserved for her care.

> Investigate the costs of residential care options in your area; this can give you an idea of what you can afford and help you decide what is possible and if a move sooner or later is your best option. Talking with a financial advisor can help. In some areas, there are health care professionals who can help guide you through the maze of possible residential care options, costs and locations that can meet your relative's needs.
> (See *Locating Residential Care Homes.*)

○ **Leaving a home and all it represents.** Many older adults have lived in their homes for a long time; some have raised their families there.

> Allow yourself to experience sad feelings that may arise, but acknowledge and remember that life is full of change. Fortunately we have our memories and mementoes to remind us of happier times.

○ **Media depictions of long term care.** Many of our beliefs and fears about long term care are shaped by the negative stories we hear on TV, read in the newspaper, or hear from friends or other caregivers. In addition, some family members' vision of residential care homes may be based on a grandparent or older relative moving to an 'institution' many years ago.

Make an appointment to visit some care homes. Talking to staff, learning about activities that are offered, and seeing the environment may help you see how different some care homes are from what was available in the past. Many of the memory care communities and smaller care homes are now more homelike and less institutional than they were years ago.

○ **Concern that no one can care for her as well as you have.** This is often true and you will not find one-on-one care in residential care settings. On the other hand, some people with memory loss actually function better in a setting with more people and activities, when there are caring and consistent staff available.

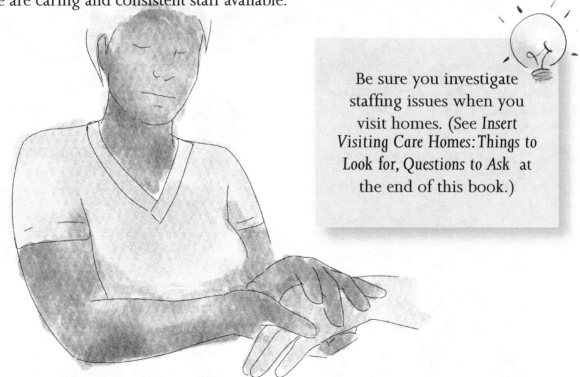

Be sure you investigate staffing issues when you visit homes. (See Insert *Visiting Care Homes: Things to Look for, Questions to Ask* at the end of this book.)

Some Things to Keep in Mind as You Struggle with this Difficult Decision

There are no clear rights or wrongs whether to move or not move your relative. If you weigh the pros and cons of various alternatives, you will likely find there is no totally positive outcome. You may feel you are making the least negative choice of all your options.

Here are a few pros and cons to get you started. Add your own thoughts.

Staying Home vs. Moving

	STAYING AT HOME	MOVING
ADVANTAGES	-Staying in a familiar environment -May receive better care -Honoring promises	-Social and recreational activities available -24 hour supervision available
DISADVANTAGES	-May be too expensive -Care is too difficult -Home is no longer safe	-Feeling like a failure -Care may not meet expectations

You are not alone. When care partners talk to other caregivers about their experience in moving a relative, they often find they share the same feelings. For many people it is reassuring to be able to talk about these difficult feelings with others who understand. Support groups are a good place to do this.

Caregiving does not end when you cross the threshold into residential care. You will still be a caregiver, although your role will be different - the staff will be the ones providing the day-to-day care. After a move, you can be an important part of the care team, helping the staff learn about your relative's background, interests, needs, care, etc. In addition, many care partners enjoy resuming their role of being a son, daughter, or spouse and not solely a caregiver.

Making the Decision to Move: When is it Time?

Thinking about moving your relative is often the first step in emotionally preparing yourself for a move that might (or might not) happen soon or in the future. As we mentioned in the previous section, **the decision to move is complicated as it involves not only emotions, but practical issue**s such as how, when, and where. Knowing when other families 'knew it was time' may help you in your decision.

As dementia progresses and a relative requires more help and supervision, care partners often ask themselves "When will it be time to move my relative?" There is not a single answer as much of the decision depends on your personal situation. **Not every caregiver has the same set of problems and not every caregiver finds the same problems stressful.** Some families keep their relative at home longer as it makes them feel less guilty. Financial resources can influence a family's decision: if there are limited resources, families often postpone the decision to move their relative and take advantage of day programs, ask family and friends for support or hire a home care agency or private caregiver to help. However, the cost of daily care or care in the home several hours a week can add up quickly.

When Rita was diagnosed with Alzheimer's disease, she told her family that she wanted to stay at home as long as possible, but she didn't want to burden them. "If my care gets too much for you, I will understand that you may need to move me to a home." As Rita's Alzheimer's progressed, her daughter Sally felt she could not keep up with her mother's care. Over the course of several months, Sally took her mom to visit five places. After each visit, Rita would say, "That is a nice place. I will think about it for later, not now." Sally soon realized that she and her brother would have to make the decision for Rita, not with her.

On the other hand .. Possible advantages of an earlier move:

⊙ In the earlier stages a person with dementia who is living at home may be socially isolated and uninvolved in activities. Difficulty initiating activities is normal as dementia progresses and may lead to depression which may worsen cognitive decline. Care partners often do not have the time or the energy to do activities with their relatives at home because of other work, family or caregiving responsibilities. In a residential care setting, where a variety of activities are offered, people with dementia can join activities with other residents with whom they may develop friendships. When people move in the later stages of the disease, they may not develop the same kinds of relationships.

⊙ At earlier stages, people may be more able to learn their way around and become used to the routines in the new setting.

⊙ Moving earlier may allow your relative to build relationships with care staff, housekeepers, dining and life enrichment staff. Care staff will know them and be able to gradually help them adapt to their changing needs. When people move in the later stages of disease, staff may view them differently since they never knew them as active, communicative people.

What Care Partners Say about Why They Moved Their Relatives

"When I felt my relative was no longer safe."

A person's abilities to recognize and react to unsafe situations diminishes over time, requiring care partners to provide more supervision. Care partners are often overwhelmed with monitoring their relative's safety: fear they may walk away during the day or night and not know how to get back home, leave doors unlocked, welcome strangers into the home, use kitchen knives or tools unsafely, etc. Keeping a relative safe 24-hours a day, 7 days a week can be emotionally and physically exhausting.

(See *Staying or Living Alone: Is it Safe?*)

"When I could not keep up with my other family and work responsibilities."

As dementia progresses over months or years, the care partner often takes on some of the responsibilities that their relative can no longer do. Taking on these new responsibilities while providing care for someone with memory loss in addition to other work, community and family duties can often be overwhelming.

"When I could not keep up with the care that she needed."

Of course, this can mean different things to different families. Some families find it stressful to cope with changes in behavior – repetitive behaviors or questions, sleep, wandering, helping with dressing, bathing, toileting, etc. Some families find it difficult to take on the tasks that their relative can no longer do: shopping, managing money, managing medications, meal preparation, housekeeping, arranging and attending doctor appointments, etc. Taking on these tasks is often gradual. Care partners often find that they do not realize how much they are doing for their relative and how it is affecting them both physically and emotionally.

(See *Caregiver Responsibility Chart in Staying or Living Alone.*)

"When my health was affected and I felt at risk of being injured providing the care she needs."

As we have said throughout this book, the care needs of a person with dementia – Alzheimer's disease, Lewy Body dementia, or strokes – increase as their disease progresses, often putting care partners at risk of injury or harming their health. Care partners frequently will go to great lengths to keep their relative at home, including sacrificing their own health.

Questions to think about:

- **Do** you feel your caregiving role has affected your health?

- **Have** your friends, family or doctor expressed their concerns about all you are doing,

- **What** is the effect on you physically and emotionally?

Sandy was able to keep her husband at home for several years after he was diagnosed with Alzheimer's disease. At first, he required minimal care. When his dementia progressed and he needed help in the bathroom and with dressing, she felt she was wearing out, but she was determined to care for him at home as long as possible. One night he fell out of bed and could not get up. Sandy tried to lift him, but she was afraid of injuring her back and called 911 for assistance. "This was my wake-up call. Even though my doctor had been telling me for months that I needed to move Sam, I didn't want to believe that I couldn't care for him at home." She was now ready to explore residential care options.

"When my family told me I needed to move him."

When family members are in agreement about moving their relative to residential care, moving is often easier. When family members disagree about keeping a relative at home vs. moving her, it can lead to tension in the family about whether moving is the right things to do.

Try having a family meeting led by a health care professional, if you are not sure what to do or if there is disagreement among family members. A facilitator could be a nurse, social worker, spiritual leader, attorney or in some cases a good family friend. She can include everyone in the conversation: what each family member's understanding is of their relative's current situation, about their feelings related to moving their relative, the demands on the primary caregiver, and how all family members are coping with their relative's changing abilities and needs. The facilitator can also offer assistance, reassurance and guidance in making the moving decision.

"When keeping him at home with the amount of help he needed just became too expensive."

As previously mentioned, there are programs and services in many communities that can provide respite for the care partner and social and recreational opportunities for the person with memory loss. Unfortunately, most of these programs are private pay. However, it is worth asking if they offer scholarships or a sliding scale.

"When my relative did not recognize me anymore."

As Alzheimer's disease and other types of memory loss progress, a person usually loses the ability to consistently recognize family members or friends. This loss can make care partners feel they have lost the connection to their relative.

"When my relative no longer recognizes home."

As Alzheimer's disease and other types of memory loss progress, a person may eventually stop recognizing home. Sometimes this results in the person constantly asking to go home or trying to leave the house to find home.

"When my relative needed more assistance with personal care tasks than I could handle, especially incontinence."

Some families report that helping their relative with personal care tasks such as bathing, dressing or incontinence is uncomfortable. Assisting a relative with incontinence can be an especially difficult emotional task.

Albert had been able to keep his mother safe at home and give her the care that she needed for the past few years. When she became incontinent, Albert told a fellow caregiver, "I just can't do this part. It just doesn't feel right for me to have to clean up my mother's urine and bowel accidents. She doesn't want me to have to clean her up and I don't want to do it. I think the professionals can probably take care of this easier than I can."

Locating Residential Care & Understanding The Finances

After receiving a phone call from her mother's neighbor, Nancy realizes that her mother is no longer able to live in her apartment by herself. According to the neighbor, Nancy's mother, Mabel, has been hibernating in her apartment for several months. When she does come out she is not always able to find her way back without help. Nancy flies to see her mother and confirms the neighbor's concerns about Mabel who also appears to be losing weight. Nancy returns home, knowing that she must find a place nearby where her mother can live safely. Where does she begin?

Locating Residential Care Homes

First, Learn the Types of Care Available in Your Area
Terminology and regulations for residential care homes differ from state to state. The different types of housing have different names, regulations and financing depending on the state in which you live.

- **Assisted living may**
    - include national corporate chains or local organizations;
    - be stand-alone or part of a retirement community;
    - be large buildings with 40-50 residents or small buildings with 6-10 residents;
    - be regulated or, in some states, unregulated;
    - be profit or non-profit;
    - include a specific memory care unit or may not.

- **Small group homes** - sometimes called adult foster care or board and care homes - are regulated as assisted living in some states and are a separate category in other states.

- **Memory care** - also called dementia care or Alzheimer's care - may be
    - stand-alone or part of a larger assisted living or retirement community;
    - a separate licensing category or may be considered assisted living or specialized assisted living.

- **Nursing homes** are known as skilled nursing facilities or convalescent homes in some states. Nursing homes are generally for people who have medical needs that cannot be taken care of in assisted living or memory care communities. If a person has limited funds, or is on Medicaid, the only option may be a nursing home.

The diagram below shows a continuum of residential care options, from living independently to being dependent on others for personal and medical care. Nursing homes are the most regulated and usually the most expensive.

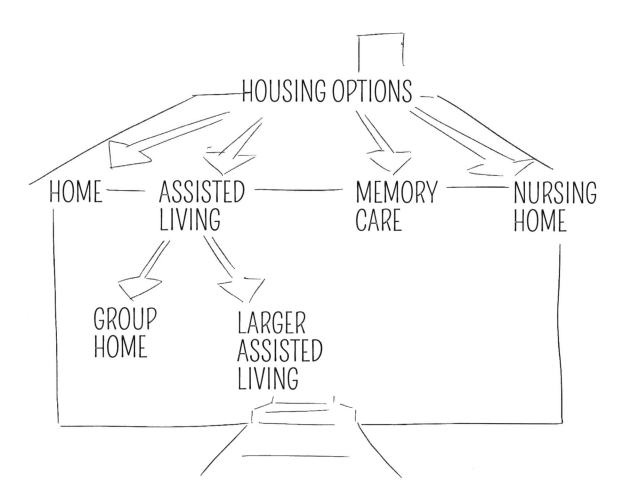

You may also find this booklet helpful in thinking about options:

eldercare.acl.gov/Public/Resources/Brochures/docs/Housing_Options_Booklet.pdf

Find Out What's Available in Your Area

There are many available resources to get you started:

⚬ Contact your Area Agency on Aging (AAA). Staff at the AAA can help you understand the different types of housing in your area. You can find your AAA through the website below.

eldercare.acl.gov/Public/Index.aspx

⚬ Contact your local Alzheimer's Association. They also have lists of available housing and can help you understand the different types of housing in your area.

www.alz.org

⚬ Hire a geriatric care manager. Care managers work privately and will charge a fee but often are great resources for local options. Find one through

www.aginglifecare.org

⚬ Contact one of the placement services available online. These are usually private businesses with local experts or self-employed independent placement consultants. They can talk to you about care options and what places have vacancies. Often there is no cost to families because the consultant is paid a finder's fee by the residential care community you choose. Some placement specialists may be familiar with some but not all options for people with dementia.

⚬ Look online for specific kinds of housing, keeping in mind that not all places advertise online.

⚬ Ask friends who may have moved a family member or know someone who has.

⚬ Ask members of a local caregiver support group, your church or other community.

Be aware that most referral sources will not make recommendations, though they may be able to help you narrow your search based on criteria such as the following:
- Geographic location
- Cost
- Appropriate level of care. This depends on many factors. See *Assessing Your Relative's Level of Care* on the next page.

Assessing Your Relative's Level Of Care

When you contact different providers to inquire about services for your relative, you will likely be asked about her activities of daily living (ADLs). This worksheet can help you describe what your relative can do for herself and in which areas she may require partial or total assistance.

EATING	DRESSING	GOING TO THE BATHROOM	BATHING	MOBILITY	FALLS & HOW OFTEN
independent	independent	independent, continent	independent	no difficulty, good balance	not aware of any falls
needs a little help	needs a little help	incontinent, manages independently	needs a little help	uses a walker or a cane	falls once a month, or so
needs supervision & prompting	needs supervision & prompting	needs reminders and a little help	needs supervision & prompting	needs assistance walking & getting in and out of bed, chair, toilet	falls once a week, or so
requires extensive help	needs help with all aspects of dressing	incontinent day or night	needs assistance and cooperates	uses wheelchair independently	falls daily
unable to do task alone	resists even though she needs it	incontinent day & night, needs assistance, but resists	needs assistance, does not want others to help	uses wheelchair, not independent	unable to get up by self

If your relative is being discharged from the hospital:

Speak to the discharge planning or social service department. However, be aware that hospital staff do not always understand the long-term care needs of patients with dementia or may not be up to date on housing options. They may, however, be able to refer you to a placement service, independent specialist or a geriatric care manager.

Figure Out What You Can Afford and Learn How Financing Works

Where your relative will end up living will depend to some extent on the financial situation. Each kind of residential care has its own payment structure. Nursing homes are usually financed differently from assisted living facilities which may be different from small group or board and care homes. It is important that you find out the terminology and the payment structure in your state. The following websites will assist you:

.www.aboutassistedliving.org

Medicare.gov has much more in-depth information; do an internet search for "medicare coverage for nursing homes."

While there are some differences from state to state, generally it is important to understand the following:

Ꙩ **MEDICARE** does not pay for long term care for people with dementia. Medicare pays for hospital and rehabilitation care, but not for the long term day-to-day needs of people who have progressive memory loss. Medicare is a federal program.

Ꙩ **MEDICAID** (Medi-CAL in California) is a combined state and federal program with some commonalities nationwide but many differences from state to state. Medicaid is for people who are low income or have used up most of their assets. Medicaid pays for a great deal of the nursing home care that is given to people with dementia who cannot afford nursing home rates privately. Although most assisted living care is paid for privately, in some states Medicaid may help with some of the costs.

It is often wise to consult a family or elder law attorney with Medicaid expertise to make sure you understand your legal situation. Medicaid is very complicated. As a spouse or partner, it is very important that you understand how Medicaid works in your state. There are special financial considerations given to spouses, but again they differ from state to state. Sometimes it is important to set up a trust but there are different kinds of trusts which a Medicaid-savvy attorney can explain to you. Also, be aware there are "look back" periods in most states. This means that if you are applying for Medicaid for your relative, their finances (and yours if you are married) will be scrutinized going back a certain number of years (the look back period). If you gave money away to relatives or others, you may be disqualified from Medicaid for a certain period of time.

Be aware that in many cases assisted living is private pay. When the money runs out, residents are often asked to leave and may have very few options at that point. There are many factors to weigh in making this important decision.

If you have a Long-Term Care Insurance policy, pull it out and read it carefully. Some people have been paying on an insurance policy for decades, thinking they are covered for all contingencies. When the time comes, they sometimes find that there are many limitations or restrictions on coverage. Not all policies cover day programs or assisted living, for example.

Looking At Care Homes With Or Without Your Relative

Mary lived alone in her home. She had managed quite well until recently when she got lost walking to her son Bill's home 3 blocks away. She was not eating the meals that Bill brought her and the medications that her son set up for her each day were not always taken. Bill knew it was time for her to move. He tried talking with his mother about visiting a couple of places, but she became angry at him and said "I will NEVER EVER leave my house. I am fine here and take care of myself." He found a care home, made the deposit and wanted to take her to visit before the actual move, but he was afraid if she knew ahead of time, she would not move. What was the right thing to do for his mother?

Many care partners like Bill find it very hard and uncomfortable to make the decision to move a relative with dementia without involving her in the decision. It often is the first time they have made a decision without the input of their spouse or parent. The decision whether not to or to visit places with a relative before moving is a very individual one. It may be helpful to talk to the move-in coordinator. She may be able to assist you in deciding if visiting before the move is a good idea. Keep in mind that some residential care homes may not have previously had a prospective resident visit before moving in. Other care partners, and friends can also help you make this decision.

Here are some things to consider in making this decision:

Your relative's awareness of the level of assistance she needs. If your relative lacks insight into how much help she needs, it is likely she will not feel she needs to move and a visit beforehand may not have many benefits. Visiting can also increase her resistance.

The extent of your relative's memory loss.
Some individuals' memory loss and disorientation is so severe, a visit may not be worthwhile.

Oliver called his son, who lived a long distance away and told him he could no longer afford the increasing hours of home care assistance his wife Jenna needed. Jenna was severely confused and they thought a visit beforehand would confuse her more and have few, if any, benefits.

On the other hand, some people in the earlier stages may be able to be involved

For 3 years Vincent had been caring for his wife at home. As her care became more challenging for him, he wondered how much longer he would be able to care for her without jeopardizing his own health. Vincent and his daughter talked to her about visiting a home they liked and she was agreeable to visiting it. They looked around and when they left, she said, "I never want to live there. I would not like having dinner with 30 other people." As they were leaving, she asked Vincent to look at smaller care homes.

Your family's ability to support her after the visit. Some individuals who are moderately to severely confused may not remember the visit, but may feel angry or unsettled afterwards. She may or may not be able to explain why she feels this way. It can take time and energy to calm and comfort a relative when she feels this way. If she is more resistant, how will that affect you? Your moving plans? How do you think your visit will affect her between the time of your visit and moving day?

Past experiences and conversations. It may help to think about past conversations about moving. Has your family talked about this? If so, what was your relative's reaction? Although these past conversations may be helpful in deciding whether to take her to visit, it may not be a good predictor of how she might react to moving.

In Summary:

Possible Benefits of visiting with your relative

- It involves her in an important life decision.

- It may help relieve your guilt, especially if she is involved in the choice of places.

- The new home may be familiar and comfortable to her when she does move.

- Visiting acquaints her with the environment and staff.

- You can observe her reaction to caregivers and residents.

Possible drawbacks to visiting with your relative

- It may cause or increase
  - Confusion
  - Agitation during and after the visit.

- She may have a negative reaction.

- Your visit may affect her between the time of your visit and moving day.

- Your relative may need extra support and attention from you if she is upset or more confused.

- She may not remember the visit.

- She may get upset at seeing more impaired people.

Visiting Together After A Decision Has Been Made:

If you decide to introduce your relative to the care home before moving day, here are some suggestions that may help you:

Plan the visit during your relative's best time of day. Your relative may be more comfortable and receptive to visiting with you if the visit is scheduled during the time of day when she is rested and has had a good meal. If your relative takes medications for pain, plan your visit after she has taken her medication(s).

Inform the move-in coordinator ahead of time. Explain that you have told your relative about the visit and what she understands (or doesn't) about the move. For example, if you have told your relative that you are going to a place that you just learned about, you do not want a staff member to say, "Welcome! We are so glad you will be living here!" Tell the staff person what might be comforting and upsetting for your relative to see or hear.

Keep your visit short. The length of your visit should not exceed your relative's tolerance to be in an unfamiliar place. Watch for signs that she may be ready to leave: facial expressions, a change in behavior or level of agitation, or indications she is in pain.

Plan your visit around an activity or a meal. Your relative may be more comfortable visiting during an activity that you can do together, and she will enjoy. Think about what she responds positively to - Social times? Music? An art project? Bingo? This might take advance planning, so talk to the staff person who is organizing your visit ahead of time.

Observe your relative's reactions to the residents. Your relative may expect to see residents who are much like her. She may be taken back seeing moderately to severely impaired residents. Watch your relative's facial expressions and body language. Does she appear concerned, anxious or scared? If so, ask the staff member to take both of you to a quiet area and talk to you about events and activities that are offered.

When Ellen took her dad to visit, she was expecting him to be angry. Although he was not happy to be there when they arrived, he became more interested in the residents and the environment as they walked around the building. He saw a few men playing checkers and asked if he could watch them. Ellen felt reassured that her dad would have things to do and make new friends here.

Contributed By

David Troxel, MPH is a writer, speaker and dementia care consultant based in Sacramento, CA. With Virginia Bell, he is co-author of six influential books including the Best Friends Approach to Dementia Care (Health Professions Press, 2017, second edition). He has been a family care partner to his mother Dorothy who passed away with Alzheimer's disease in 2009. Read more about his work at www.bestfriendsapproach.com and follow him on Facebook at www.facebook.com/bestfriendsapproach.

David Troxel, MPH

> *Great memory care programs involve three key areas: people, program and place (the physical environment).*

*I*n today's connected world, it's easy to choose a restaurant for a great night out.

Go to the restaurant's website and study the menu. Read the online reviews from a variety of sites; often there are hundreds of comments. Decide if the prices fit with your budget. Begin to get excited about an entree or dessert that seems especially enticing.

All this information helps us make a better (and hopefully delicious) choice.

If only choosing a residential care program was as easy! Company websites begin to look alike, and generally present a positive view of life in memory care. There are a growing number of online comments, but it often seems that the reviews are all over the map. Pricing information is rarely available online. Helpfully, many states have data bases that publish citations received from surveyors, but even good places get citations now and then.

What to do?

Great memory care programs involve three key areas – people, program and place (the physical environment).

Let's look at the people – the staff

When visiting a memory care program take note of the staff demeanor. Do staff members greet you as you walk by, smile, seem energetic? Do you witness caring and loving interactions between staff and residents? Do the staff seem to like each other and work as a team? Staff are trained to be welcoming to potential families on tour, but you should still be able to feel authentic emotions and energy.

As you are touring, ask the Marketing Director or Executive Director about staff longevity (or look at the nametags since many companies post the number of years employees have worked). This is an industry where there is significant turnover, but hopefully you will see plenty of seasoned team members.

Ask about staff training – how does the company teach staff about current trends and basic care? Does it seem minimal or more impactful? Progressive companies go above and beyond the basics to create a culture of learning that helps their employees succeed.

Assess the program

Without truly effective medicines for Alzheimer's disease and other dementias, the current "treatment" for dementia is socialization. When residents with dementia are active and live in a community that encourages caring relationships, happiness goes up and behavior challenges go down. I like to say that the brain loves company. Therefore, it is important to choose a place or program for your family member that has a rich array of activities.

> The current "treatment" for dementia is socialization.

Look at the monthly calendar. Does it have personality? Ambition? I like calendars that have some playful and interesting language; instead of "exercise class," how about, "Let's Get Moving." This proves more inviting to residents and suggests a creative spirit on the part of the activities team.

Are activity staff present seven days a week? What are the hours? Hopefully staffing in this critical care is robust.

Does the program encourage more spontaneous activities? As you tour take note of whether staff are sitting to have a cup of coffee with residents, giving a hand rub, or engaged in conversation. These 30-second moments add up!

How is the food? Is there a resident kitchen available for cooking activities? Many states don't allow residents living in a memory care community in the kitchen, but sometimes there is a resident kitchen for cooking activities. Can your mom have her favorite snacks throughout the day? If the building has multiple levels of care, do you sense that the amenities and food are of similar quality to independent living?

A few specifics about activities – contemporary dementia programs embrace music, exercise, time spent outdoors and activities that offer purpose (baking dog biscuits for the local shelter or making centerpieces for a cancer support program). Many programs also use the Internet to travel the world virtually (taking a tour of the Louvre in Paris, France) or to visit a resident's home town. Look for activities that match abilities of residents at all levels.

Another key element of the program is staff's **use of resident Life Stories**. Because residents may have forgotten much of their past, it's important for staff to know them well to provide cues and to celebrate past achievements. Ask about how staff learn life stories. You want your mom's care team to know that she won a national prize for her pumpkin cheesecake, loves animals, speaks three languages, or raised 4 children. Knowing these things allows staff to make a better connection and to do or say just the right thing on more difficult days.

Observe the physical environment

Many newer memory care communities are beautiful and offer a country club level of amenities. Living in a beautiful space clearly has its benefits, but I've seen great memory care in church basements and not-so-great memory care in palaces!

When considering a place for your family member, look for a place that pays attention to its environment. Little things matter to me since they can reflect a lack of organizational focus on memory care or skimpy budgets. Are there weeds in the garden when you are touring – empty spots without mulch? Is furniture and carpeting clean or damaged/stained? Many companies, including non-profits, may not have the resources to buy new furnishings every year but you still want to see a team that takes pride in the basics.

Does the community smell nice and look clean? Many residents with dementia are incontinent—accidents do happen—but you want to choose a place that is on top of basic care and cleaning.

Is there outdoor space that is inviting? I think it's important to be out of doors to experience the sensory and spiritual benefits of nature. Look for raised beds or nice chairs and paths in the garden space.

How is the lighting? The older eye needs better lighting; hopefully there aren't too many shadows and the community has lots of natural light to provide brightness and a connection to the out of doors.

Ultimately, **does the place feel like home**? Is it a place that promotes community and conversation, friendship and fun?

Choosing residential care for a family member is one of the most difficult tasks and can be emotionally wrenching. I spoke with a husband recently who told me that he felt that he had "surrendered" his wife when he moved her into memory care; he said he was suffering from tremendous guilt.

These feelings are understandable but as we sat and talked I shared my own story about my mother's move into memory care and how the socialization and friendship had been so healing and therapeutic. She enjoyed almost all of the daily activities and made new friends. A fluent French speaker, she even taught French vocabulary lessons to some of the staff!

My father and I were able to have fun with her on our visits, while getting help from the staff in her personal care.

Most families provide significant care in the home before ever making a placement and this can work when there is a strong family network or when you find in-home workers who are lively and engaging. However at a certain point it may just become too difficult to keep someone at home. In these cases, be assured that most people with dementia moving into assisted living or residential care settings do well and many even thrive with the good food, inviting activities and enhanced sense of community.

Note: The worksheet, Choosing a Care Home: Things to Look for, Questions to Ask, (p. 163) *lists David's suggestions and other things to look for when visiting a care home.*

Other Kinds Of Moves

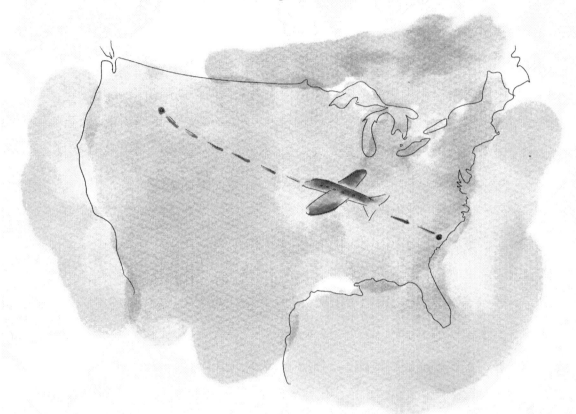

Moving A Relative From Out Of State

If you have time to plan, there are things to do ahead that will make the move easier.

"When we were moving my mom, I wrote out a list of things that our family needed to do. 'Operation Mom' was a great communication tool and kept our family on track."
– Jeff, caregiving son

Ahead of Time

Know the housing options and the level of care your relative needs.
(See *Locating Residential Care* and *Assessing Your Relative's Care Needs*.)

Medical Records

Obtain all medical records from all of your relative's doctors (primary care physician, neurologist, other specialty doctors such as cardiologist, pulmonary or orthopedic doctors, etc.) There may be a charge for copying and transferring records.

> º If your relative belongs to a large multi-state system with a shared electronic record system, such as Kaiser Permanente, you may not have to do this, but it is a good idea to check.

Obtain dental, optical and audiology records.

Obtain hospital records, such as test results, scans and x-rays.

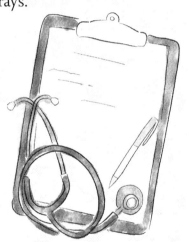

Medical Care

Try to find medical care ahead of time: a primary care doctor, a neurologist and other needed specialists. The Alzheimer's Association, the Area Agency on Aging or a geriatric care manager may be able to tell you what doctors are accepting new patients and if they are known to work well with patients with dementia.

Check to see whether there is a geriatric clinic or physician in your area. That may be the place to start.

Make sure the new doctors accept Medicare and your relative's insurance. (You may have to get new health insurance in a new state.)

Medications

Refill all medications ahead of the move. Get a paper or digital list of current prescriptions.

> ○ Be aware that you may not be able to fill prescriptions from out of state, hence the need to have enough medications.

Change address for national pharmacies or on-line pharmacies.

Check with local pharmacies in the new state to see what they will need or whether they have access to old records. (Large national chains usually can see old records online.)

Bank Accounts

Leave old accounts open until a new account has been established to receive Social Security checks and other direct deposits.

Open a new account in the new state. What will the bank require to set up a new account? Do you need proof of Durable Power of Attorney?

Change address on checks.

Social Security

Notify Social Security Administration of the address and bank account changes. Keep in mind it can take weeks to months for Social Security to deposit checks into the new account.

Investment accounts

Check with your relative's investment advisor to see whether changes need to be made on the accounts. It is the law that financial advisors be registered in the state where their clients live. National firms, such as Schwab, do not require changing accounts, as most of their brokers are registered in multiple states; this may not be the case for independent brokers.

Insurance

Investigate Medicare Insurance. This is particularly important for Medicare Advantage and Prescription Drug plans. Most "Medicare Supplement" plans provide coverage anywhere in the USA without the need to make a change. However, the cost of the plan will likely change when a person moves. Two sources that offer help if your supplemental insurance has to be changed:

- Your Area Agency on Aging

- The State Health Insurance Assistance Program (SHIP) helps "Medicare beneficiaries make informed decisions that optimize access to care and benefits."
www.shiptacenter.org

Forward the mail. You can do this on line or in-person.
moversguide.usps.com

The US Post Office recommends you do this 2 weeks - 3 months before a move.

Medic Alert bracelet/Safe Return: Notify them about the address change:
alz.org/help-support/caregiving/safety/medical-alert-safe-return

The Out Of State Move Itself

Moving is always hard. Moving a relative across state lines can be particularly challenging. There are many things to consider as you approach this, including the following:

Driving considerations:

> ᵒ If it is a long drive, can your relative tolerate it? Have you traveled together recently so that you have an idea about how it will go?

> ᵒ Be prepared for bathroom stops and be sure you keep track of your relative in rest areas.

> ᵒ Do you need to spend the night en route? If so, think about safety considerations in a motel or hotel.

> ᵒ Be sure you have all the documents you need: list of medication; identification; emergency contacts; travel information.

Flying considerations:

Virginia did not understand that they were going on a trip. About 2 hours into a 4 - hour trip, she became increasingly restless and upset which was disturbing the passenger sitting next to them as well as all the passengers around her. The flight attendant was able to move a person out of her row to give her more room, brought her snacks and gave her a pillow and blanket. Her husband wished he had been more prepared and had asked her physician for a sedative.

○ **Medication**: We do not normally advocate medications, except as a last resort. However, when a long car trip or plane ride is planned, it may be helpful to have a sedative available. Virginia was most likely frightened and felt trapped.

○ **Wheelchair service makes the airport much easier,** even if your relative walks well. This service is generally free, although you might want to tip the transporter. You must make the arrangements ahead of time and it should show up on your relative's reservation. There are different levels of help – they will need to know whether your relative can walk onto the plane unassisted. Advantages include: your relative is seated and can't wander off; assistance is usually provided by a transporter who helps expedite going through security and can assist with carry-on bags.

○ **Avoid short layovers.** If at all possible, take direct flights, but if you have to change planes, make sure you have adequate time. Often people with wheelchair service are the last passengers off the plane.

○ **If incontinence is an issue,** think through bathroom stops at airports. Look for family bathrooms, which are large, separate rooms where you can accompany your relative. Do you need to double the incontinence briefs? Do you have spare clothing in your carry-on luggage?

○ **Consider your seat assignments**. if your relative has mobility issues or is incontinent, and you can afford it, consider asking for an upgrade. There is much more room, you will be closer to the bathroom and you will receive more assistance from the flight attendants.

○ **Arrange for someone to meet you at your destination.** Having an extra pair of hands to help with baggage and getting your relative settled in the car will be very helpful and reassuring.

Getting Settled

Get a new state ID card. Eventually you may need to prove residency in the new state. Every state is different about regulations for issuing new ID cards, so find out what the rules are in your state. Usually this is through the department of motor vehicles.

Elizabeth tried to get a new ID card for her mom. They went to the department of motor vehicles in the new state four times. They needed two pieces of mail that had her new address in the new state. They also needed an original birth certificate which she did not have, although she had a copy and an expired passport. Elizabeth's mom was repeatedly denied a new ID card. Eventually she was able to get a new ID card from her previous state, which had looser regulations. It had the old address, but at least she had a picture ID.

Learn about Medicaid regulations in the new state if you think your relative may eventually need to be on Medicaid. Remember that Medicaid is a federal-state partnership and every state has different Medicaid requirements. Things to keep in mind:

- Consulting an elderlaw attorney about Medicaid requirements in the new state may be helpful. If your relative has a lot of assets, the attorney can also help you think through planning financially for long term care.

- If you need help finding out about Medicaid or about other insurance options, contact your Area Agency on Aging

www.eldercare.acl.gov
or
www.n4a.org

- If your relative was on Medicaid in her previous state, you must close out coverage in the old state, before applying in the new state.

- You will need to prove residency in the new state, which means you may need to get a state ID card.

- Financial and medical eligibility can differ from state to state.

- If your relative needs to be on Medicaid immediately after the move, fill out the paperwork in the new state ahead of time so that it can be submitted as soon as the move is complete.

Legal Documents

- Decide whether there will be a change in powers of attorney for health care or finances because of the move. Whether or not the people change, you may need to get new documents. There is not uniformity among states in terms of legal documentation. You may want to consult an elderlaw or family attorney.

Medical Appointments

- Schedule appointments with the new physicians to establish baseline care.

- Do you need a handicap sticker? Most states require a doctor's statement and a photo ID before a handicap sticker can be issued by the DMV.

Moving A Relative Into Your Home

John moved into his son Alexander's home after his wife died suddenly. John had a diagnosis of Alzheimer's disease and could not drive anymore but did not want to move across the country to Alexander's. He was worried about disrupting their family with active thirteen-year-old twin boys. And he was sad to leave his church community behind. Although he lived with them for more than a year before moving to a small group home, it was a difficult year. John felt the family patronized him. Alexander's wife, who did not work outside the home, felt that John had been "dumped in her lap." The boys were reluctant to bring friends home because Grandpa John was always in the family room. Overall, it was not an easy move.

Marilyn's mom came to visit Marilyn and her husband and, after a month, asked if she could stay. The guest room where her mom stayed was near a bathroom that had grab bars and a walk-in shower. Marilyn's mom could negotiate the whole ground floor with her walker and did not have to deal with the steps she had in her own home. Although she loved her house, she recognized how much easier it was to live at Marilyn's. For a while, she was able to help with meal preparation and simple household tasks, but gradually there was less that she could do. She became resentful when Marilyn went to her part time job, and Marilyn felt too guilty to go out with her spouse or friends. Eventually they found a companion who Marilyn's mom enjoyed, which made everyone happier.

If you are thinking of moving a parent, sibling or other relative into your home, there are many things to consider. If at all possible, it can be very helpful to talk this through ahead with a counselor, spiritual adviser, a close friend or another caregiver who has had similar experience.

Moving a person with progressive dementia into your home will change your lifestyle in multiple ways. Some things to keep in mind as you plan include:

Is everyone in your home on board with this decision?

> ° Sometimes there is no choice, but it is really important that everyone in the home is listened to prior to the move.

How will your relative view the move?

> ° Will she feel uncomfortable as John did in the example above?

> ° Again, there may be no other options at this time, but listen to and acknowledge your relative's feelings.

Will everyone in the family be able to have some privacy when needed?

> ° How will you do this? It is important to talk about this ahead of the move to avoid family members feeling resentful that they cannot access the kitchen, have friends visit or watch TV when they want.

How much supervision will your relative need?

> ° Look at *Assessing Your Relative's Level of Care* for an idea of the kind of help needed currently.

> ° Will you be able to handle all the tasks yourself? Will you need to hire help?

> ° Remember that with a progressive dementia, your relative will gradually need more care and supervision.

What is the physical environment of your home?

> ○ Are there adaptations that need to be made to make it safe? Installing grab bars? Removing throw rugs? Increasing the lighting in the bedroom and hallways?

> ○ Review the home safety checklist from the Alzheimer's Association:
> www.alz.org/media/Documents/alzheimers-dementia-home-safety-checklist-ts.pdf

Marilyn, from above, discovered that her mom could not get up from the armless dining room chairs without help, resulting in several falls. Marilyn bought a comfortable office chair with arms so that her mother could safely get up and down by herself.

Can you accommodate some of your relative's old routines? Food preferences? Hobbies?

> ○ While this is not always needed or possible, these things may help your relative's adjustment. Routines in particular become very necessary and important for individuals with dementia.

Are there relatives available or resources to hire someone to stay in your home occasionally so you and your family can get away?

> ○ Some adult children who offer to take a parent into their home negotiate with siblings or other relatives for regular respite breaks.

Are there financial considerations?

> ○ Will you be using your parent or sibling's finances to make this work? Is your relative comfortable with that?

> ○ Are there other family members you need to discuss this with?

You may have friends or family to talk to when times become difficult. Will your parent (or sibling) with dementia have someone to talk to?

⚬ Think about creating opportunities for your relative to be able to talk privately or socialize with someone if she chooses. It could be a home care companion, a phone call with an old friend or sibling, or it might be someone at an adult day program. While your relative may not need this, many people in this situation do need the opportunity to discuss their new living situation with someone other than you.

Have legal documents and decisions been put in place?

⚬ Who has financial power of attorney for your relative? How will that impact this arrangement?

⚬ Who is the health care advocate /durable power of attorney for health care for your relative? How will that impact this arrangement?

⚬ Do these legal documents need to be redone with this new living arrangement?

Can you bring some of your relative's favorite furniture or objects into your home to help her feel more at home?

⚬ Read *The Move*, the next section in this book, for more ideas about preparing and helping with adjustment.

Contributed By

Grace Lee, LCSW, ACSW, is a Geriatric Case Manager at the Senior Health and Memory Center, Kaiser Permanente Santa Clara Medical Center in northern California. She has served on the Board of the Alzheimer's Association of Northern California and Northern Nevada and worked at the University of Michigan Geriatrics Center and Alzheimer's Disease Research Center. She has also been a care partner for her mother, Stella, who died from Alzheimer's disease in 2016.

Grace Lee, ACSW

Mr. Jones, age 80, lives with his wife in their home. He has multiple medical conditions in addition to Alzheimer's disease. He recently tripped and fell in the back yard and his wife called 911. In the ER, they discovered he had a hip fracture that required surgical repair. He was hospitalized, and after a successful operation, he developed a fever and became more confused and disoriented and did not remember what had happened to him. He was very weak and could not get out of bed without a great deal of assistance. He was also not able to remember the precautions to follow to protect his recovering hip and did not cooperate with the physical therapist to begin rehabilitation while at the hospital. His wife felt overwhelmed with the dramatic changes she observed in her husband's behavior. She was relieved when he was discharged to a skilled nursing facility for rehabilitation and recovery.

It is not uncommon for a person with dementia or memory loss to become hospitalized. An unexpected fall or accident may require a visit to the emergency room, resulting in hospitalization. Other health issues may cause the person to become ill and require hospitalization. These situations cannot always be avoided, but preparation and knowing what to expect can help make it easier for the individual and their care partners.

Some Things to Know

⚬ **Conditions that cause the person with dementia to be hospitalized can lead to a temporary or long term decline in cognition.** The unfamiliar and busy environment of a hospital, the presence of unknown individuals and uncomfortable procedures, may result in considerable upset and stress. These factors may worsen confusion and anxiety and cause the person to yell out and sometimes strike out at others.

○ **Even a seemingly minor illness, like a bladder infection, can cause a major change** in the person's cognitive, physical and mental functioning. Our brains are our command centers and function to help us stay oriented, think clearly, respond appropriately, and be able to perform everyday activities. An illness or injury can disrupt this functioning.

○ **Delirium is the term for severe confusion and disorientation which occurs unexpectedly.** Problems such as fever, infection, dehydration and chemical imbalances can cause delirium, resulting in acute mental status changes that may occur rather abruptly, resulting in extreme confusion and disorientation that can have negative outcomes for patient and family. A high percentage of people with dementia experience delirium in the hospital. It is not always recognized as delirium by hospital staff since they do not know the person.

○ **Find out about your relative's status: Is she an inpatient or on observational status?** An overnight stay in the ER or hospital does not always mean your relative is considered an inpatient at the hospital. It is important to ask what your relative's status is: Inpatient or Observation Status. Although your relative may actually be in a hospital bed, if she is categorized as observation status, then she is considered outpatient. This means that she will be responsible for co-pays and deductibles (Medicare Part B) that would not apply if she were inpatient (Medicare Part A). It's very important to clarify this.

○ **The hospital status may affect how much you pay for certain hospital services** (for example, lab tests, x-rays, and drugs). Most importantly, it may also affect whether Medicare will cover care in a skilled nursing facility (SNF) following their hospital stay. Normally, you need to have a 3-day inpatient hospital stay in order to qualify for Medicare covered care in a SNF after hospital discharge. Observation Status days don't count toward the 3-day stay rule. Medicare Advantage Plans sometimes have different rules, so once you know your relative's status, check with your insurance company about coverage and co-pays.

○ **Hospital care is best thought of as a choice.** Think ahead about what you and your family might do if your relative is injured or becomes ill. If the person is in the advanced stages of a disease and the primary goal is to keep her as comfortable as possible with quality of life most important, it may be appropriate to talk about whether home based care is possible or if hospice care may be a better option.

Preparing for Hospital Emergencies: Things to Think about Ahead of Time

○ **Planning ahead** can sometimes make hospitalization easier, but you cannot completely prevent all problems.

> *Medical facilities are not usually designed well for those with memory loss. Staff should be informed that the person has dementia (preferably not in front of the person).*

○ **It is essential that a trusted person go with and stay with the person in the Emergency Room (ER).** A trip to the ER can be frightening and disorienting to a person with Alzheimer's disease or other memory loss conditions. Medical facilities are not usually designed well for those with memory loss. Staff should be informed that the person has dementia (preferably not in front of the person).

○ **Be prepared to give a history of your relative's accident or illness, as well as her limitations.** As the individual may not be able to give a good description of her symptoms or history, the care partner should be prepared to clarify what led up to the decision to seek emergency evaluation and treatment.

○ **Identify some back-up help in case the ER wait is a long one. Do not leave your relative alone in the ER.** People are not necessarily seen in the order in which they come to the ER, but by the nature and severity of their condition. It is ideal to identify a couple of dependable family members, neighbors or friends who can come at short notice, so any forms or paperwork can be handled while someone stays with the person with dementia.

○ **Work to stay calm, positive, and reassuring, and be prepared to provide comforting words and gestures.** How you feel and express yourself will often be noticed and reacted to by your relative. This can be reassuring if you stay calm, or it can cause increased anxiety and upset if you appear anxious.

○ **Be prepared for a long wait and for multiple staff members asking the same questions repeatedly.** Laboratory tests, x-rays and other procedures will lengthen the time before a treatment plan can be identified.

◦ **Your relative may or may not be admitted to the hospital.** If you feel that your relative needs to be admitted for more thorough evaluation and treatment, try advocating for hospital admission. This doesn't always work, but it is worth a try. Also, ask for the social worker who works in the ER; she can help advocate with you. This means you want more of a workup and treatment, usually when someone seems too ill to come home.

◦ **Do not leave the ER without a clear understanding of what you are supposed to do**, how to monitor your loved one's condition, how to provide needed care, and when to arrange for follow up.

What to Bring to the ER or Hospital

Ahead of time, put together a packet "Things to take to the hospital" that you can easily locate:

◦ Health Insurance Cards including Medicare, Medicaid/Medi-Cal
cards and supplemental insurance or HMO
or Medicare Advantage plan cards;
◦ A summary list of all known health conditions including Alzheimer's disease or other form of dementia;
◦ List of current medications, both prescription items and over the counter, including the name, dosages and frequency of use;
◦ Allergies and adverse reactions: to drugs and foods;
◦ Healthcare provider names and phone numbers;
◦ Copy of advance health care directives or health care proxy (documents that state who the designated health care decision maker is and what health care wishes the person may have, especially for end of life care);
◦ Do Not Resuscitate (DNR) forms if appropriate.

The following items may also help you during your relative's time in the ER or hospital:

◦ Packable snacks and a water bottle or beverage for yourself
and your relative;

⍥ Pad of paper or notebook and pen to jot things down, such as directions given by hospital staff or notations of your relative's symptoms or problems and any questions you may have;

⍥ Cell phone and charger/battery to help you call or communicate with family and others;

⍥ Change of clothing for patient and any disposable adult briefs and hand wipes;

⍥ Glasses and hearing aids for yourself and your relative;

⍥ Reassuring comfort items, such as a pillow/blanket, photo album, reading material, or enjoyable music with earphones.

How to Help During the Hospital Stay

> Help hospital staff understand the person's normal functioning and behavior.

Don't go it alone. If possible, build a small care team of family, friends and possibly a paid caregiver to support your relative, especially if she is expected to be in the hospital for more than a couple of days. It is important for the care partner to have adequate support and rest to cope well and be prepared for the increased support the hospitalized person may need.

Try to promote your loved one's normal routine while in the hospital. Ask if regular medications can be continued and about **potential side effects of any new medications.**

Help hospital staff understand the person's normal functioning and behavior. Ask them to avoid using physical restraints and medications to control behavioral changes if at all possible, as these may worsen confusion or behavior. Try to have someone who knows the patient stay at the hospital at all times, especially during medical tests and procedures. This may be hard to do, but will go a long way to help keep the person calm, and less frightened, and less likely to try to leave.

Bring sudden changes in behavior or confusion to the immediate attention of hospital staff. This may be delirium. You may not recognize or understand your relative's behavior. For example, she may not realize she is in a hospital or may be having hallucinations or delusions that are upsetting to witness.

Working with the Health Care Team at the Hospital

Teach staff how to communicate best with your relative. Staff may have limited training and experience caring for a person with dementia, so be prepared to help them talk and interact successfully with your loved one. For example, tell them what words you are using to explain to your relative what is happening. Ask staff to be sure to tell your relative what they are doing or going to do. If there are special issues such as vision or hearing loss, it will be important to explain how best to cope with this.

Help ensure patient safety by informing staff about any prior issues with wandering, getting lost, falls, paranoia and any delusions/hallucinations.

Be patient, but don't hesitate to be an advocate for your relative and politely ask for what is needed or explain your concerns. Remember that hospital staff are caring for many people.

Start thinking about preparing for the hospital discharge soon after admission.
o What is the goal of the hospital stay and the desired outcome? Be prepared to ask staff questions about what to expect.
o Every hospital has staff designated to help patients and family members prepare for discharge. Find out who on your patient's care team is responsible for this. This person may be the bedside nurse, a nurse case manager/discharge planner and/or hospital social worker.

Prepare for your loved one with dementia to at least temporarily need an increased level of care and support after discharge. Be ready to ask what services are available to supplement your own efforts - home health care such as skilled nursing, physical and occupational therapy, or medical equipment. It is also not unusual for people to become so weak during a hospital stay that some time in a skilled nursing facility for short term rehabilitation is beneficial. **Remember that your relative must spend 3 nights as an in-patient in order for Medicare to pay for a Skilled Nurse Facility (SNF).**
o Be sure to find out what insurance coverage is available or not for any of these options. With support and guidance, your loved one and you can leave the hospital at discharge with the knowledge and ability to transition back home or to the appropriate next level of care.

Ask for the support you need. If the situation becomes overwhelming or stressful, or you need help advocating for your loved one, you should feel free to ask for help from the hospital social worker on the unit. If you are concerned about being able to take care of your relative, even with help, speak up early and often to identify options such as in-home caregivers, or community care options such as adult day care, assisted living communities, or board and care homes.

Resources

Going to the Hospital: Tips for Dementia Caregivers by the NIH National Institute on Aging. www.nia.nih.gov/alzheimers. 1-800-438-4380.

Tips for Hospitalization. Memory and Aging Center. University of California, San Francisco. https://memory.ucsf.edu/tips-hospitalization.

Alzheimer's Association. 24/7 Help Line. 1-800-272-3900. www.alz.org

The Move

Talking With Your Relative About The Move

As we mentioned earlier (see *Why Moving is Hard*) most people in the later stages of dementia may not be included in the decision to move because of their level of cognitive impairment. Even when families understand that this is their only option, they often feel guilty and confused about how to talk to their relative about the pending move. There is not one "right" way to do this as each person and family are unique and have different needs and characteristics. If you are unsure who, how and when to tell your relative here are some tips that may help you.

What should I say?

Plan what you are going to say. Take some time and write it out. Rehearse it with another family member or friend, if needed. Think about how your relative might react and prepare what you will say if she asks questions or becomes upset.

Tell her what she will understand. Decide how honest and direct you will be in talking about the reason she will be moving. Some families are more comfortable telling their relative a partial truth if it makes their relative feel better. Other families are not.

Who tells her?

Generally speaking, the person should be someone your relative knows and trusts. Who does your relative listen to?

A relative. Some people with dementia may be more receptive to hearing about the move from a relative. Some families decide to have more than one person tell her. Consider if more than one person is involved if your relative will feel "ganged up on." Other families decide it is better to have only one person there and have other family members be available later to support her.

Someone outside of the family. Others may accept the news better from a friend, health care professional, or a spiritual leader.

A doctor is often asked to tell his patient that she can no longer stay at home. Call her doctor and tell him why you think she needs to move: she is unsafe, you have tried other options but they have not worked, your health is at risk, etc. Make sure the doctor knows that you have the legal authority to make the decision to move her.

At the appointment ask the doctor to write out why she needs to move on a prescription pad. You can refer to this if she asks later why she has to move. Keep in mind that some doctors will do this and some will not. Some doctors may ask that their patient be informed of the move prior to the appointment.
(See *Sample Letter from a Health Care Professional*.)

As Gladys' dementia progressed, her daughter Ellen, asked Gladys' long time doctor to talk to her about moving. After the discussion, he handed Ellen a RX pad "You are not safe at home anymore. It is time for you to move." Gladys did not like it, but she did agree to move. After the move when Gladys said, "Why am I here? I want to go home", the care staff showed her the doctor's note and it calmed her down for a while.

When is a good time to tell her?

There is no right time to do this. It depends on many factors including your relative's ability to understand and cope with what she will be told.

If you think your relative will be shocked, allow enough time to listen and offer reassurance.

Pick a good time for your relative. When is she most rested? Comfortable?

Often thinking about a past event when she was agitated before an event can help you determine how long in advance to tell her about moving.

Think about telling her 24–48 hours ahead of time if you think she, and you, need more time to be emotionally and psychologically prepared.

When Jerry thought about when to tell his wife, Jackie, that she was moving, he remembered one time when she had a doctor's appointment and he told her the day before the appointment. Jackie paced the whole day and throughout the night. She was so anxious in the car on the way to see the doctor that Jerry had to turn around and go home. The next time she had to go see the doctor, her told her right before the appointment and this did not upset her. Recalling this incident, Jerry felt it would be best to tell Jackie the morning of the move.

How do we tell her?

Keep it simple and be consistent. Too many details can be confusing. When more than one family member is involved in the moving talk, it is best for everyone to tell her the same thing.
(See Sample Script for a Family Meeting)

Acknowledge her feelings. If your relative expresses sadness, anger or resistance, tell her "I know this is hard for you. This is hard for me too."

Mike and Mary came up with a plan of how to tell their mother that she was moving. The day before moving day, they sat down with her and told her, "Mom, we do not think you are safe alone anymore. Dr. Rich agrees. We found a place that we think you will like and you can move in the apartment tomorrow." When she repeatedly asked 'why', they would both repeat the same words.

Watch for a change in your relative's mood and behavior. It is not unusual for a person with memory loss to react to the move with resistance. Although this doesn't always happen, sometimes a person with dementia can become more confused, angry or agitated when a move is imminent.

Will a change of mood and behavior continue after the move?

Again, this varies from person to person. Some people do not react strongly to their new surroundings. When a new resident feels secure with the people and place, she may be more accepting than the family expects. (See *Common Emotional Reactions for New Residents*)

Sample Letter by a Health Care Professional

A variation of this letter could be provided during a doctor appointment or sent afterwards to reinforce a discussion that was held during the appointment.

Dear Mr./Mrs./Ms.

I enjoyed seeing you again in my office several weeks ago. I am writing now to recommend that you no longer live alone in your home at this time. Due to your health conditions, it is much better for you to live somewhere where there are people to cook meals for you, assist with your medicines and other parts of daily life.

It is extremely important for you to live somewhere right now where you can be with other people and participate in a variety of activities. The socializing and activities with other people will help keep your mind and body healthier. I understand that your daughters have found an excellent place that offers all these things. My recommendation is that you move there for now so that you have access to all these services.

I know that your children are very devoted to you and are taking good care of things for you.

I look forward to seeing you at your next appointment.

Sincerely,

Sample Script for a Family Meeting

This was a handout at a family meeting with a man with Alzheimer's disease and his adult children. He had been asked to move out of his independent apartment after he started knocking on other apartment doors in the middle of the night.

He could still read and understand simple documents. It was printed in a large font and read to him at the meeting by the facilitator. Family members had reviewed this before the meeting and discussed how they would respond to his questions..

Insert names or change wording as needed.

Why you have to move:

- You have an illness that is affecting your memory and sometimes causes you to be confused about things.

- Because of this illness, your doctors feel you need to be in a different place with more help available.

- There are two very nice places – you can choose between them. Your son will take you to visit them.

Why is this happening?

- This is not anyone's fault. You have an illness that is making your memory and thinking not work as well as they used to.

- It's not unusual to feel angry about this. But please understand, this is not your children's fault. They are doing their best to love and support you.

What will happen?

- You have a choice of two places to move where more help is available when you need it.

- One choice is _____.

- _____ is another choice.

- Both places are full of kind people with good intentions. It will be an adjustment for you, but you will be fine.

Moving a relative with dementia requires some planning. Dividing the task of moving into 3 phases can help you feel less overwhelmed. Here are some things for you to consider as you prepare for the move, moving day, and adjusting to the move.

Preparing for the Move

> "When our family was faced with moving our mom, we created a list of things to do and each of us was responsible for doing several of the jobs. This was a great communication tool and kept us on track." - A caregiving son

Complete all the paperwork ahead of time, if possible.

If there is paperwork that needs to be filled out on moving day, ask how long it will take and what your relative will be doing while you complete the forms. New residents can be anxious after arrival when they are not with their relative.

Ask what to expect.

This is a new experience for your family and knowing what to expect ahead of time can help you feel more prepared. How long will the move-in process take? Who will greet and escort you and your relative to your relative's room? What happens next?

Try to schedule the move at your relative's best time of day.

When is she most rested? In the best mood? Is there a time of day when she is at her best physically and cognitively?

Plan how you can help your relative feel more relaxed on moving day

It may cause less confusion and fatigue to follow your relative's routine on moving day. On the other hand, doing something special such as going out for lunch or getting her hair done may help her feel more relaxed before she arrives at the care home.

Ask someone to go with you

It can be comforting to have someone other than the move-in coordinator with you and your relative during the move-in process to help you get settled.

Decide if your relative can be involved in choosing what items to take

Simplifying this task may allow your relative to be involved in the decision of what she wants to take and what she wants to leave behind.

While their mother was out for lunch with a friend, Matthew and his sister put red sticker dots on the things they thought their mother would like to have in her new room. When their mother returned, they showed her what they thought she would like to have with her. She chose one more item and then said, "OK". This allowed their mother to be included, but not overwhelmed in deciding what to take.

Put together a photo album or collage

A photo album is a nice way to document a person's life and provides staff with things to talk about with her. Label photos with dates, names of people and location: "At our lake cottage with Grace and Joe, 1942."

Plan what you will do after you leave your relative at her new residence

A great deal of planning and emotions went into this day. Some caregivers feel they need time alone as they enter into this new chapter of caregiving. Others need to be with a friend and do something enjoyable: take a walk, go out for dinner, etc.

Prepare notes for staff on how to answer your relative's questions/concerns

Your relative may ask staff "Why am I here?" "Why can't I go home?" It can be helpful to write specific answers to questions that new residents often ask. Ask the staff representative to share information with all staff members.

- What to call her new home. How you have described where she is moving: an apartment, room, a place that helps people with memory problems, name of residence, etc.

- How long she will be there. A while, until she feels better, it is up to her doctor, etc. Giving her one of these answers does not sound so final and may give her hope she might return home while she adjusts to her new place.

- What staff can say if she repeatedly asks for you or another family member. "Your husband will be here this afternoon, tomorrow, soon, etc. He knows that you are here, etc. "

- What things NOT to say, things that will upset her. "This is your home now. You are going to be living here from now on. "

Linda's doctor thought it best for her to move to Sunflower Care Home "while her medications were being changed." Linda agreed, thinking she would return home in a few months. The staff member, who welcomed her, said, "We are glad you will be living with us." Linda said she would only be there a short while, but the staff member said, "No, this is your new home." Linda became agitated and very angry hearing that she would not be going home again.

Moving Day

The feelings that you experienced during the planning period may be more intense on moving day. On the other hand, you may not feel the full emotional impact of moving your spouse, parent or friend until after she has moved.

- **Be prepared for mood swings.** Feeling sad, relieved, anxious and guilty are normal and can even be expected. Whether your relative understands the move or not, it may be emotional for you.

- **Recognize that plans may go astray.** Despite your best laid plans, it is not always possible to follow a schedule for a person who is confused and forgetful. For example, your relative may get up later than usual on moving day, causing you to be late in arriving at the care home. Try to be flexible and calm.

- **Dedicate the entire day to moving.** Although moving in will probably not take all day, families often feel tired after the move. If possible, try not to schedule other appointments or activities. Spend the rest of the day caring for yourself.

- **Depend on staff to help you.** Staff are used to helping families with various feelings and aspects of moving. Ask staff if you need privacy or need extra help to get oriented to being in the building. These feelings are not uncommon. These are very common requests.

○ **Introduce yourself to staff.** These are going to be important people in your relative's, and your life. When staff don't know who you are, they often feel uncomfortable. (See *Building Relationships with Staff*.)

○ **Decide how long you will stay on moving day.** The move-in coordinator may have some suggestions for you. Keep in mind, however, it often is hard to predict how long you should stay, as much depends on how the move-in process goes. Sometimes a longer stay only postpones the departure; sometimes it is necessary to provide comfort and reassurance to your relative. Some families move their relative in before lunch, leave for a few hours and come back for dinner and to tuck them in for the night.

○ **Plan your departure.** If you expect your relative will be angry or want to go with you when you leave, ask staff to help you with your departure. They can be quite creative in supporting you and the new resident at this time.

○ **Ask whom you should call for an update.** Find out who is the manager on each shift so that you can call and check in if you wish.

○ **Ask if you can spend the first night with your relative.** If you feel your presence will help her feel more comfortable the first night after she moves, ask the home if you can stay with her. Keep in mind that your relative may misinterpret this gesture and think you are going to stay more than one night. Not all homes have the space, nor allow family members to stay overnight.

○ **Plan your next visit.** Let staff know when you will be back for a visit. Try to schedule your visit within a few days after the move, if possible. (See *After the Move*.) Call before you visit and ask if this is a good time for your relative to have a visitor.

When Mel moved to Red Maples Memory Care, his wife, Ginger, was concerned about his adjustment. He understood that he had to move and was sad, but he often hallucinated and became frightened. Ginger asked permission to sleep on a futon on Mel's floor for the first couple of nights. She would go home for part or most of the day but return to spend the evening and night with him. This made a huge difference in Mel's adjustment to Red Maples.

Adjusting To The Move

Common Family Feelings After the Move

After struggling for months with the decision to move her husband Steve, Diane and her children moved him to a care home. Although she planned every step, Diane found that once Steve moved into the care home, she felt confused about him being there.

"Moving was harder than I could have imagined. I have had moments when I have second guessed my decision. Is the care good enough? Especially the first morning when he looked at me and said, 'Can you get me out of here?' "

I try to remember what Steve's doctor told me: "Your husband needs more care than you can give him. He needs to move to a place that can give him the assistance and care that he needs." His permission was what really made me move Steve, and now when I think of his doctor's words and encouragement, it makes me feel better, but it continues to be a roller coaster ride: some days are hard for me and some days I feel nothing but relief. I expect it will take a while before both of us settle into this new chapter of our lives.

Despite the careful planning and the support that Diane received, she felt confused about her decision and what she was feeling. It may help you to understand common and natural reactions to this significant transition.

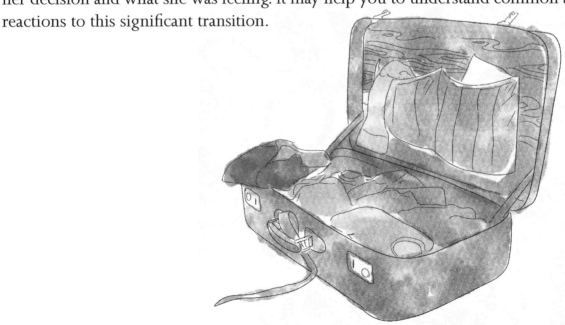

Guilt

is the most common reaction to moving a relative with memory loss. Many care partners feel guilty, thinking that they "should" have been able to care for their relatives longer despite their inability to do so for the reasons discussed throughout this book.

Think about what you are giving her: more opportunities to be with others, to engage in activities and to be in an environment that will keep her safe and where she will receive 24/7 care.

Know that the feeling of guilt usually lessens over time, as you and your relative become more comfortable, adapt to the new routine and environment and get to know the staff and other residents.

Think about what you have given her in the past: comfort, time, help. Tell yourself that you did the best you could. Sometimes care partners forget all the things that they provided for their relative as the disease progressed. You can continue to provide comfort, and support in the new setting.

Uncertainty and anxiety

Care partners often ask, "Have I done the right thing?" "What happens if it doesn't work out?" It may help to remind yourself that this is a new experience for both of you. It may take some time to adjust to the differences in the care she is receiving now versus when she was at home with you.

Recognize that anxiety is a normal reaction to a new experience that neither of you have gone through before. Often families have to get through the experience of moving and the adjustment period before they can feel confident in their decision. It can take up to 3 months for the new resident to adjust to an unfamiliar place, routine, and care staff. Anticipating this may help relieve your anxiety.

Talk openly to people who have supported you through this illness and in this decision: friends, your doctor, pastor, rabbi or fellow caregivers.

Talk to the appropriate staff person about how your relative is adjusting. Your anxiety may be a reaction to hearing your relative say "I want to go home," when you visit her. Ask when your relative is least and most anxious. Sometimes new residents act differently during visits than during other parts of the day.

Talk to your doctor if you feel a level of anxiety that is interfering with doing things, your relationships, your sleep, or your health. Anxiety can be very disabling, or it can be part of depression. Consult your doctor for an evaluation.

Grief

You may find that the move intensifies grief, especially, sadness and anger.
Grief is a natural reaction to the loss of taking care of your relative, to witnessing her changing abilities, and to the changing role for you, the caregiver.

Let yourself experience the feelings. It is better to feel the sadness or anger than to fight it. It can help to talk to other caregivers who have been through the moving experience, friends or other family members.

Try to do one enjoyable activity each day following the move. Research has demonstrated that taking positive actions can improve one's mood.

Know that feelings of grief usually lessen with time.

Failure

Care partners sometimes feel like a failure after moving their relative because they feel they did not try hard enough. This is rarely the case. Most care partners dedicated love, energy, and time to caring for their relative, sometimes for years.

Tell yourself that you did all you could. Sometimes caregivers forget all the things they did and how hard they tried to keep their relative at home. If you kept a journal, take some time to read it. Check in with family and friends about how you are feeling. Think about all the changes and challenges that you experienced over time and the situations and problems you dealt with and problems you were able to solve.

Congratulate yourself for being flexible, caring and hardworking and doing your best. No one can make this disease go away.

Keep in mind that very few caregivers are able to maintain their relatives at home until the end of life. The *Alzheimer's Association Facts and Figures* (2018) quotes a figure of 75% of people with dementia are admitted to nursing homes by age 80 (page 50).

Fatigue

An enormous amount of physical and emotional energy is required to care for a person with dementia. This may be the reason that you moved your relative. Coping with the move and the adjustment to it, can deplete your energy even more.

Try to recognize that you may not have the energy to do all the things that you normally do. It takes time to recover emotionally and physically.

Get some rest. It is common to have a difficult time sleeping, but if this goes on for weeks, talk to your doctor. Problems with sleep can be part of grief, but also one sign of depression.

Be aware that fatigue can affect your cognitive abilities - attention span, memory, orientation - and put you at risk when doing routine tasks such as using tools or driving, for example.

Relief

Relief may or may not be an expected reaction after the move, but it is not uncommon. You may feel relief that others are involved in the care of your loved one. On the other hand, you may feel ambivalent about sharing the care. Or you may feel relief quickly followed by guilt. You may never feel relief. More likely, you may not feel relief until your relative has adjusted to the move.

Common Emotional Reactions for New Residents

In the first few days, Joe felt lost, confused and asked repeatedly, "Why am I here?" Several times a day, he told the staff he wanted to go home. He spent much of his time in his apartment packing his suitcase so he could be ready to go home when his wife visited. He slowly began to settle in over a period of several weeks.

Joe's story is not uncommon, however, keep in mind there are great differences in how residents react to living in a new place. Some people will adjust easily, while others will have a difficult time understanding why they are there and why they can't go home. It may be helpful to prepare for some of the common reactions that new residents experience in the adjustment period.

Grief

Any move – whether voluntary or involuntary – is usually perceived as a loss. Transitioning from a familiar home to a new place, having others assist you in making decisions, adapting to a new routine and caregivers contribute to a loss of control and other feelings. Although this may show up in unexpected ways for people with dementia, most of the reactions listed below may well be part of your relative's grieving process.

Confusion and disorientation

All of us feel a little confused and disoriented when we move. This is more pronounced in people with dementia because they may not understand why they are in an unfamiliar place with 'strangers'. They may not remember where they are. If your relative moved after an illness or being in the hospital, you may see much more confusion than before the illness. Usually this improves with time.

Try regular walks to the dining and activity room or outside to the garden. Talk about the things that you see along the way. This may help orient your relative to her new surroundings.

Point out landmarks along the way to her room. Doing this regularly during the initial days after the move can help your relative find her room and some of her belongings.

Anxiety and agitation

These feelings often increase and often go hand-in-hand in the initial period after moving. Some new residents feel anxious because they feel lost not knowing what they should do or where they should be. For people who are in the later stages of dementia, these behaviors may be the only way they can tell you that they are upset.

Remind yourself that anxiety and agitation usually decrease as a person adjusts to her new surroundings, staff and routine.

Try telling your relative that she is safe, and you know where she is.

Try to remain calm when your relative is anxious. If you are concerned about your relative's behavior, ask the appropriate staff person if the level of agitation or anger is normal given the time she has lived there.

Think about what might give her reassurance.

Listen. Sit with her. Tell her you know that this is hard for her and you too.

Every night Toni would get agitated when it was bedtime. Toni felt calmer when staff showed Toni her son's photo along with his note: "Mom, I love you. I am happy to know that you are there. I will visit soon." Your son, Jay

It is common and understandable for new residents to say, "I want to go home." Although you may be tempted to take her home for a visit, it may not be in her best interest. A visit home may cause increased agitation and set back her adjustment. Ask staff for their opinion about taking her home or on an outing.

Anger

is a very normal reaction to a move, especially when it is against a person's wishes or without her prior knowledge. Sometimes an individual expresses anger towards family members, making for uncomfortable visits and feelings of guilt.

Listen. If it becomes too difficult to listen, change the subject or involve her in an activity such as a walk, having a snack, etc.

Acknowledge her feelings. Saying "I am sorry you feel this way" may be helpful.

Try not to argue about why she needs to live there or talk her out of her anger. This usually does not work, for either of you!

If nothing works, consider shorter visits. Sometimes longer visits prompt agitation and anger during the adjustment period.

Sadness

It is natural to feel sad or overwhelmed about the newness of everything.

Ask the appropriate staff person if the changes you are seeing are within the normal range for new residents.

Feeling lost

Your relative may feel as though she doesn't belong, have anything to do, or know anyone. Feeling comfortable doing activities or being with others may take longer than you expect.

> Talk with staff how they might involve her in activities.

> Help staff think about what she enjoys and doesn't like to do. If you are concerned about how your relative is doing, ask for a care conference. At this meeting, staff – often the management staff and a caregiver assigned to care for your relative - will talk to you about how your relative is adjusting. If staff are not available to attend a care conference, ask for a private meeting with the Director or Care Coordinator. Care conferences are required within a certain number of days after a resident moves in some states; in other states, it is only required, in certain types of housing.

> **Staff were constantly trying to get Edna to come to Bingo. When they urged her to come with them, Edna became angry and agitated. When her daughter told them that Edna viewed Bingo as gambling and against her religion, staff offered her an alternate activity which she enjoyed.**

Keep in mind that most people with memory loss do adjust. The amount of time it takes new residents to adjust varies greatly. Some new residents adjust quickly, others take longer – up to 3 or more months to acclimate to their new surroundings

Visiting After The Move

Many care partners feel uncertain of what to expect and what to do during the first few visits. (*See Emotional Reactions for New Residents.*)

"I didn't sleep at all the first night after my mother moved in. I had so many thoughts and feelings. She was angry when I left her, and I feared she would be even angrier when I visited her for the first time. If she asked how long she had to stay there, I didn't know what to say. I didn't know how to tell her she wasn't coming home. I felt guilty that she had to move because I could no longer manage her care. When I visited her for the first, I found my mom in her room, talking to one of the care staff with a smile on her face. She told me that she had slept well and was looking forward to doing some of the activities that were offered today. Not all the days were as smooth as this one, but overall, my mom accepted and adjusted quite well."

"The day after my dad moved into the care home, I visited him right before lunch. He met me at the door, with his bags packed and ready to go home. I tried to explain why he needed to stay here, but he wouldn't listen. It was a difficult conversation because he didn't understand why he couldn't go home. After a while, I left in tears, wondering if I did the right thing in moving him."

As these experiences illustrate, new residents' initial adjustment can vary greatly, depending on the many factors we have mentioned throughout this book.

> "My brother and I had planned a visiting schedule so one of us would visit mom every day for the first couple of weeks. When we told the Director what days and times we would visit, she told us that their policy was "no visitors for the first 10 days so new residents have time to adjust to their new routine and surroundings." I was confused as I knew that mom would be confused about where she was. I wanted to be there with her to support her during this transition."

We start this section with an important, but controversial point.

Sometimes families are told by a memory care community that they have a "no visit policy" for the first few weeks while new residents adjust.

We disagree with this policy for several reasons:

- **It is unknown** how an individual will react to living in her new home, as the stories above illustrate.

- **This policy suggests** that all residents
  - **adjust in the same way,** which we do not believe to be true, as the two stories above illustrate.
  - **adjust better and more quickly** to their new surroundings without visitors.

- **In our experiences,** not having visitors can cause a new resident to feel abandoned, hopeless and frightened. Family visits can give their relative reassurance that they love them and know where they are.

However, an exception might be made if your relative is extremely agitated after your first few visits. Then it may be reasonable for staff to request that you visit less often, make visits shorter or postpone visiting for an agreed upon period of time.

We suggest you ask the care home what their policy is before the move, so you can prepare for your first visits, or question this policy very carefully.

Initial and ongoing visits

First visits.

Call before you visit. Ask the director or supervisor if this is a good time to visit.

Keep your visits short. Your relative may tire easily, have a short attention span and may not have an accurate concept of time – how long you have been there or how often you visit. Fatigue, agitation, and change of mood may be signs to end your visit. Tell the staff who will visit in the coming days or weeks.

Keep the numbers down. Too many visitors at one time can be overwhelming for people with dementia. Be sensitive to what works for your relative.

Keep in mind that the feelings inspired by your visits are more important than the content. Visits don't always go as planned, but sharing a pleasant moment, even though your relative may not remember it is what counts.

Learn to modify activities as your relative changes.

At first Eleanor's mother could still write simple emails to friends and family as long as Eleanor pulled up the email and sat with her. Gradually her mother lost the ability to type but she still enjoyed talking about the content and telling Eleanor what to type. Eventually, Eleanor would write a note to family and friends and read it to her mother before sending it. Sometimes she showed her mother a photo of the person they were emailing. Although her mother could no longer initiate these activities, she still enjoyed being part of the discussion.

What Makes Visiting Difficult?

"When she is angry at me
for putting her there without her permission,
even though she participated in the decision."

"Keeping the conversation going
when she is quiet or not in a good mood."

"When she is upset, and I can't understand what she is saying."

"When she is overly anxious or upset."

"When she wants to go home."

"When I can't make it better for her."

"When I prepare to leave, and she gets angry or sad."

"When she is not responsive, and I see her going downhill."

"When she doesn't recognize me."

What Makes Visiting Successful?

"When I can share a story or an experience with her."

"When I walk in and she smiles at me."

"When she recognizes me."

"When she is comfortable and content."

"When she likes the gifts that I bring her."

"When I see her interact with the other residents or staff."

"When we join an activity group together."

"When she is ok when I leave."

Max dreaded visiting his wife, as she no longer was able to stay focused on conversation. He began keeping a bag in the car with things that might interest Matilda. Some days he would take out several framed photos to look at together. Other days, he brought in some special music or a book. With a little planning, Max found visiting much easier.

Things to do when you visit

- Decorate her room
- Sing or listen to music together
- Look at old photos or videos
- Watch her favorite old movie
- Share stories about family, friends or events at church or elsewhere
- Take a walk
- Take a favorite food of hers.
(Make sure it will not interfere with her medication schedule)
- Enjoy a meal or do an activity together
- Comb her hair
- Apply lotion to her hands or feet
- Read a favorite poem, book or Bible passage
- Sit together. Listen to what she says
- Hold her hand. Enjoy the silence

Some helpful websites with more visiting ideas and tips:
iog.wayne.edu/pdf/making_visits.pdf

Visiting as Your Relative Becomes More Impaired

Many families talk about how much more difficult visiting becomes as their relative's dementia progresses. When the person is sometimes non-responsive or can no longer participate in any of the activities that you did together previously, visits can become very painful for family members. A few suggestions:

Educate yourself about late stage dementia. This is helpful for some care partners.

Understand that just being present and comforting may be the most important thing you can do.

Many of these suggestions can be adapted to visiting people in the later stages of dementia.
- Play music that brings you both some peace.
- Simple touch may be all that is required.

Talk to other care partners - at the care home, at a support group or elsewhere.

Seek counseling if it is just too hard. Grief is a big part of this stage.
- See *Making the End of Life Transition Easier.*

Contributed By

Janet Thompson, Eldercare Consultant, founded Elder & Family Options to creatively and compassionately work with elders and families to discover options and connect with resources. She has 18 years in senior living sales and marketing for continuing care retirement centers, assisted living, memory care, and skilled nursing communities. Janet developed and facilitates a CEU-credentialed program through The Conversation Project which teaches professionals how to have conversations with clients on Advance Care Directives, POLST (Physician Orders for Life-Sustaining Treatment), and End of Life decisions.

Developing Relationships With Staff

Janet Thompson, Eldercare Consultant

You choose a community

because of the care and security your family member will receive. Your strongest ally is the staff who interact on a daily basis with your family member. Most often, positive care outcomes are created with positive relationships. As you settle into your new role as a family member of a new resident, the following suggestions can help you feel more comfortable with the transition that you and your relative have made.

Build a relationship

Get to know staff names and something about them. Introduce yourself and tell them a bit about yourself: "I am Gretchen's daughter and either my brother Steve or I will be visiting daily." What might you have in common? Because the staff is assigned by shift, try to visit on different days and at different times to get familiar with all who interact with your family member.

Help the staff get to know your family member

Place captions on photographs – who is in the picture and what's happening. Attach notes to mementos and art work to stimulate conversation and reminiscing. This gives the staff something to talk about with your relative and helps them see beyond the dementia to her previous life. Share comfort routines, favorite activities and food, as well as things that upset your family member.

Mr. Samuels had always been a dapper dresser – hat, suspenders, and shined shoes. When he moved into a specialty memory care community, his family created a system to enable the care staff to help Mr. Samuels continue his preferred style. Weekly, his family would bring in seven hangers, one for each day. Each hanger contained a complete outfit: underwear, t-shirt, socks, shirt, pants, belt or suspenders, sweater or vest, and shoes. Mr. Samuels was still the best dressed gentleman in the room!

Get involved

Share your talents: music, flower arranging, reading, puzzles, bring in your parrot or dog. Join in community events, whether it's Thanksgiving Dinner or Summer Barbeque, your family member will feel more comfortable with you there.

Share your family member's special occasion with the community. Ask if you can bring your mom's favorite birthday cake to share and host a party. Be sure to ask in advance if residents have special dietary needs.

Leave special instructions and reminders in writing

Communicate with the program director, nursing, and care staff. Staff have access to a daily care plan, but can get busy with other residents, and out of the ordinary tasks may get overlooked. Create a sign written in plain language, and post it in a regular and visible location, "I will pick my mother up at 2 PM on Tuesday, and we will leave at 2:20. Please make sure she's recently been to the bathroom and is wearing her blue coat."

Learn who does what

There is an entire team of folks where your family member lives: the caregivers, as well as activity, dining, health and medication, billing, and community management staff. Go out of your way to introduce yourself and get to know them early in your family member's residency. Find out who is responsible for which area and how best to address future concerns, such as: How will a change in your family member's condition be communicated?

Complaints

A community is made up of people and, as such, mistakes happen. Who do you go to when you have a complaint?

○ The first step is to talk with the staff member who is responsible for the concern you are raising, and with whom you have a relationship.

○ Maintain your calm. Take a deep breath.

○ Put your complaint in writing – email may be the most efficient. Reread your complaint before sending. Stick to the facts as you know them.

○ Ask questions to understand why the entire situation occurred.

○ Ask for written corrective steps and an agreement to a follow up.

○ Additionally, if the concern is regarding the care or health of your family member, ask for a meeting to discuss your relative's adjustment or care. Discuss your concerns and determine what corrective steps will be taken.

⚬ As a last resort, you have the right to contact an Ombudsman, a designated person who advocates for nursing home and board and care residents. Ombudsmen provide assistance in resolving grievances and disputes. The federal government requires all nursing homes to post information about Ombudsman services in their state. Requirements for other kinds of residential care, such as small group homes, vary by state, but every state has an Ombudsman.

Trust that staff members are doing their best

If you arrive and your father hasn't had a shower, ask the appropriate staff person how his day has been before you complain. Even the most amenable resident can have a challenging day. And sometimes a staff member is sick and everyone is having to cover extra residents.

Team praise

You know how hard it is caring for a person with memory loss on a day-to-day basis. Be generous with thanks and praise for the team who cares for your family member. Who do you tell when someone has done an outstanding job with your family member?

Josie regularly visited her mother in the evening. Frequently, she brought hot egg rolls or fresh fruit for the staff to share during their dinner break.

Contributed By

Daniel Kuhn, MSW, is Vice President of Education at All Trust Home Care that primarily serves people with dementia living in the Chicago area. For more than 40 years he has been a licensed clinical social worker in various care and research settings including the Rush Alzheimer's Disease Center, the Alzheimer's Association, and Rainbow Hospice and Palliative Care. He has authored or co-authored more than 50 publications including Alzheimer's Early Stages: First Steps for Family, Friends and Caregivers. He can be reached at dan@alltrusthomecare.com.

Daniel Kuhn, MSW

L iving with dementia is challenging enough but dying with or from dementia can be even more difficult. It does not have to be this way. Good planning, communication, and education are essential to ensure a peaceful end to one's life. Otherwise, needless suffering may be created by well-meaning yet misguided decision-makers eager to use aggressive medical care aimed at postponing death. Comfort is the final gift we can offer to someone with dementia.

What causes death in people with dementia?

○ **Many people with dementia die of another illness such as heart disease or lung disease.** Their dementia often complicates the care and treatment of these other illnesses, but dementia does not contribute directly to their death. They can be said to have died with dementia while another medical condition proved fatal.

○ **Others will likely die from a complication of their dementia such as pneumonia.** Those with dementia who survive or do not have other life-threatening illnesses develop severe cognitive and functional deficits and require full-time care at home or in a care facility. They can be said to die from dementia, since dementia itself is the underlying cause of death.

○ **Some people stop eating and drinking as the brain and other vital organs shut down.** They may no longer be able to swallow, or they simply reject food. Regardless of the circumstances surrounding someone's death, all concerned must prepare for the inevitable.

The importance of advance directives and power of attorney for health care

Dementia results in diminished capacity to manage one's financial affairs and make prudent health care decisions. Appointing someone to act in one's behalf prior to incapacity is the best way to ensure that one's wishes are carried out in the future.

○ **A "Power of Attorney for Health Care" is the primary means** to protect the values, preferences, and goals of the person with dementia. This is a legal document.

◦ **Planning early while the person has the ability to make decisions minimizes or prevents disagreements** among relatives and friends about who is in charge and what decisions are to be made at a later time.

◦ **Failure to designate an advocate prior to incapacity can have dreadful consequences.** For example, who will decide if heart surgery should be performed or if kidney dialysis should be initiated? Should a feeding tube be inserted if someone is losing weight? What if the person with dementia had voiced opposition to such measures yet did not put one's wishes in writing prior to incapacity? How will differences of opinion regarding care decisions be settled among family members? A costly and contentious legal battle may ensue over who has the right to act in behalf of the person with dementia. A judge may ultimately decide who is best suited to act in the person's best interests and appoint a guardian to serve as a substitute decision-maker. The following case example illustrates the perils of poor planning:

Louise had Alzheimer's disease and counted on her husband Harry to make financial and health care decisions. When he suddenly died, their three children learned that advance directives had never been completed. All care decisions were now up for debate, but Louise's children disagreed on just about everything. When Louise was diagnosed with cancer, a legal battle among her children took place over the right course of action. A third party was appointed by a judge to be her guardian who in turn insisted upon futile medical interventions in the last months of Louise's life.

End of life decisions

Keeping people alive as long as possible is a primary goal of health care practitioners. However, that goal may conflict with the wishes of someone opposed to life-sustaining measures at the end of life. The tests, procedures, people, and places associated with traditional medical care are very confusing to the person with dementia. Rather than improving one's life, such care may cause harm. For example, it is well known that admission to a hospital greatly increases the risk of physical, mental, and behavioral changes among people with dementia. Someone with dementia may not recover from this traumatic experience and families may also suffer the effects too. Clarifying the goals of all care decisions is essential.

The questions below are seldom addressed in medical settings unless someone speaks up and acts in behalf of the person with dementia.

⚬ Will another test, drug or hospitalization make life better for the person with dementia?

⚬ Will the benefits of interventions exceed their risks? For example, is a woman with advanced dementia going to benefit by having a mammogram that may lead to more invasive tests and aggressive medical treatments?

⚬ How can the person be made comfortable with simple pleasures like food, massage, and music?

⚬ A formal meeting should be initiated with health care professionals to clarify the goals of all care decisions and to answer a basic question: what interventions can best offer comfort to the person with dementia? A concise way of summarizing a care plan meeting is to utilize a form known to all health care professionals, Medical Orders for Life-Sustaining Treatment (MOLST) or Physician Orders for Life-Sustaining Treatment (POLST).

> *What interventions can best offer comfort to the person with dementia?*

Palliative Care and Hospice Care

Palliative care. Another outcome of care plan meetings is to involve a palliative care expert. This refers to a medical specialty focused on comfort measures such as relieving pain, shortness of breath, and other symptoms associated with the end of life. Palliative care may include consultations by a single health care professional or a team including a doctor, nurse and social worker. Such services are paid for by Medicare.

Hospice care. Another benefit of Medicare is hospice which is essentially palliative care for persons with an expected life span of six months or less. Hospice organizations include teams of health care professionals and volunteers working together to ensure comfort for someone in the last days, weeks or months of life. In addition, hospice professionals prepare relatives and friends for someone's death and facilitate their adjustment after the death. Also, Medicare pays for durable medical equipment such as a hospital bed for anyone enrolled in hospice. Hospice care can be delivered anywhere – in a private home, care facility or a hospital. Some hospice organizations also have special residences for use on a short-term basis.

The manner in which people die with or from dementia is often a choice left to others. Determining what is best for an individual requires a conversation about the goals of care that should be held before decision making capacity is impaired.

There are no specific guidelines to identify when someone with advanced dementia is eligible for hospice care. However, it is generally accepted that a person is considered terminally ill if he or she cannot walk, dress or bathe without assistance, is incontinent of bowel and bladder, and cannot speak more than a dozen words. In addition, one or more of these complications must be present: aspiration pneumonia, urinary tract infection, sepsis, skin ulcers, or significant weight loss. These criteria may not always predict death within six months but are often useful in gaining admission into a hospice organization that is designed for comfort care.

The manner in which people die with or from dementia is often a choice left to others. Determining what is best for an individual requires a conversation about the goals of care that should be held before decision-making capacity is impaired. Honoring one's wishes at the end of life is a final way of respecting autonomy, promoting dignity, and ensuring comfort. Finding the right team of health care professionals who support this comfort-care approach is important for the dying person and for one's circle of family and friends.

For more information, see Encouraging Comfort Care, a free guide published by the Illinois Alzheimer's Association.

alzheimers-illinois.org/pti/downloads/Encouraging%20Comfort%20Care_SINGLE.pdf

AFTERWORD

As we have said throughout this book, not all people with dementia are alike. The type of dementia and how it progresses, as well as individual personalities, make each person's experience unique. In addition, we recognize that relationships in families can be very different and can impact how decisions are made for a relative during the progression of dementia.

We have given general and specific suggestions for care partners, but we know that not all of the suggestions in this book will work for everyone. Talking with other care partners and connecting to local service providers may give you added support and things to try.

We also want to acknowledge again the hard work and dedication that families exhibit in their caregiving roles. Caring for a person with dementia through the many years of that journey is exhausting and challenging. But there are often moments of joy shared with a person with dementia. We hope that you are able to find those moments of shared happiness. We also hope that you will remember to take care of yourself.

Wishing you the Best,

Laurie & Beth

WORKSHEET

Visiting Care Homes: Things To Look For, Questions To Ask

When you are visiting care homes, there are many things you will want to know and to ask about. We recommend that you make one copy for each place you visit. You may also want to review David Troxel's piece, before you visit, *What Does Good Care Look Like?*

NAME OF RESIDENCE: **DATE VISITED:**

ADDRESS:

CONTACT PERSON: **PHONE:**

CHECK WHAT TYPE OF CARE HOME YOU ARE VISITING:
- ☐ Assisted Living
- ☐ Memory Care Community
- ☐ Nursing Home (also known as skilled nursing facility)

Licensing

State licensing requirements vary from state to state. Some states do not require some types of residential care homes to be licensed. However, the federal government mandates that every state have a Long Term Care Ombudsman to act as an advocate for nursing home residents and their families.

	YES	NO
◦ **Is the care home licensed by the state?**	☐	☐
◦ **Can the most recent licensing report can be reviewed?**	☐	☐

◦ **Where can you review the most recent inspection report?**
On line? Website: _____

Grievances/violations listed in the latest report:

The Environment

Many of the newer assisted living communities are beautifully designed and decorated and it is easy to get impressed by the physical appearance. As the saying goes, don't judge a book by its cover. It is what is inside that is important: staff training, the activity program, etc. Also, keep in mind what is important to your relative in the past: fancy or simple décor? Large or small places?

	YES	NO
◦ **Clean and well maintained**	☐	☐
◦ **Feels calm, comfortable & friendly**	☐	☐
◦ **Walking space indoors and outdoors**	☐	☐
◦ **Cues to help residents find their room, bathroom, dining room etc.**	☐	☐
◦ **Private area for family visiting/events**	☐	☐
◦ **Well lighted**	☐	☐
◦ **No odors**	☐	☐
◦ **Your relative would feel comfortable in the environment?**	☐	☐

(She would like the décor, not too large or small, etc.)

Personal Private Space

Ask to see one or two rooms. If there are private and semi-private rooms, ask to see both.

	YES	NO
◦ **Are there private and semi-private rooms?**	☐	☐
◦ Do the rooms have adequate space?	☐	☐
◦ **Semi-private rooms - is there enough privacy?**	☐	☐

◦ Semi-private rooms - what is the procedure for:

Choosing roommates? On availability? Personalities? Abilities?

◦ What happens if the roommates do not get along?

Fees & Levels Of Care

The cost of residential care for people with memory loss can be very expensive. There often is an assessment fee for an employee to meet and assess prospective residents to make sure they meet the criteria for the care home. It is important to be forthright about what monitoring and assistance and care your relative needs with bathing, dressing, eating, etc. (See *Assessing Your Relative's Level of Care*.)

	YES	NO
Is there an assessment fee?	☐	☐

If so, what is the cost?

	YES	NO
Are there other move-in fees?	☐	☐

If so, what is the cost?

	YES	NO
Is it refundable?	☐	☐

What levels of care are available?

Ask for a price sheet for the different levels of care you are interested in. Keep in mind they might not be able to quote you an exact monthly cost until after they conduct an assessment of your relative.

	YES	NO
Independent apartments	☐	☐
Assisted living	☐	☐
Memory care	☐	☐
Skilled nursing care	☐	☐
Only one level of care	☐	☐

How is it determined when a resident requires the next level of care?

Monthly rate
Services included in the monthly rate:

Services NOT included in the monthly rate:

Fees & Levels Of Care continued on next page>

LAURIE WHITE AND BETH SPENCER

	YES	NO
○ **The care home accepts**		
Medicaid	☐	☐
Long term care insurance	☐	☐
Veterans benefits	☐	☐
Is completely private pay	☐	☐

○ **What is monthly cost for private room?**
○ **Semi-private room?**
○ **How often are care costs increased?**
Every six months?
Every year?
Not on a regular schedule?
○ **When was the last increase in cost?**

Move In And Move Out Procedure And Criteria
○ What medical forms and tests are required before a resident can move in?

	YES	NO
○ **Do they come to the home to assess prospective residents?**	☐	☐

○ Who conducts the assessment? (nurse, social worker, other staff members)

○ What medical conditions are not accepted?

○ What medical conditions or behaviors might cause a resident to be asked to leave?

○ How much notice is the family given if a resident is asked to leave?

Family Visiting Policy

	YES	NO
○ **Is a new resident able to have visitors immediately after she moves in?**	☐	☐
○ **Are there any circumstances when family members could not visit?**	☐	☐

If yes, explain:

Care Plans

A care plan is a document that identifies a resident's needs: physical, emotional, spiritual, behavioral, social and recreational activities. Nursing homes are required to hold care conferences; some assisted living homes do not.

	YES	NO
○ Is the care plan reviewed with the family?	☐	☐

If so, when?

It is a good idea for families to ask for a care conference a month or so after your relative moves in. This gives you a chance to hear from staff how your relative is adjusting and if there are any concerns. A care conference does not replace regular communication between the family and staff.

	YES	NO
○ Is a care conference scheduled after a resident moves-in?	☐	☐
○ Are families invited to attend the care conference?	☐	☐
○ Can families request a care conference at any time ?	☐	☐

Residents' Appearance

It is important to realize that there are reasons why some residents may not be dressed when you visit: late start to their day, waiting to take a bath, etc.

	YES	NO
○ Residents look neat, clean and well-groomed	☐	☐
○ Residents appear to be odor-free.	☐	☐
○ Some residents are smiling during your visit	☐	☐

(This may indicate contentment.)

Residents' Abilities

Keep in mind that the resident population changes constantly due to residents moving in and out, and to the progression of their disease.

	YES	NO
○ Many residents seem to have similar abilities as my relative.	☐	☐
○ I think my relative would be comfortable with some residents.	☐	☐

Interaction Between Staff And Residents And Vistors

	YES	NO
○ Staff greet residents by name and respond to them .	☐	☐
○ Staff appear to speak respectfully to residents.	☐	☐
○ Staff interact respectfully and caringly with residents	☐	☐
○ Staff respond patiently to residents' needs and requests	☐	☐
○ Staff are friendly to you, smile, greet you with a 'hello'.	☐	☐

Management Team

In smaller board and care homes, the owner may be the manager and on-site most of the time or there may be an appointed manager to oversee resident care. In larger, corporate owned communities, there is usually an Executive Director, and a medical professional. Whatever the size of the care home, managers oversee the daily operations and make decisions, develop policies and set the tone for the care home.

○ **Who is on the management team and what are their credentials?**

○ **How long has the management team worked together?**

	YES	NO
○ Is one manager on site at all times?	☐	☐

Staffing

There is no universal staffing standard across the country for assisted living and smaller care homes. The federal government mandates the staffing ratio in nursing homes. The minimum staffing standard is determined by each state.

The staff to resident ratio is the number of staff to the number of residents.
For example, 8:40 means there are 8 staff who care for 40 residents. Not all staff are included in the staff:resident ratio.

Shift	# of direct care staff	# of residents
Day shift		
Afternoon shift		
Night shift		

Staff Training

In our experience, the most successful caregivers are those who are not only compassionate, caring, patient and flexible, but who have also received adequate training in caring for residents with memory loss. Staff who have only had a few hours of training about dementia care may not understand enough to provide the kind of care that you want. Again, dementia care training is not required in all care settings and states.

	YES	NO
○ Are staff trained before they start working?	☐	☐
○ Are all staff trained in working with dementia?	☐	☐
○ Dementia training for staff is scheduled regularly.	☐	☐

How often?

How are staff trained (videos, small groups, etc.)?

Activities & Socialization

Like all of us, people with memory loss have the need to do things that bring them pleasure and meaning. Ask to see the activity calendar and observe an activity.

	YES	NO
○ Are there activities offered every day throughout the day?	☐	☐
○ Are activities offered to residents with different abilities?	☐	☐
○ Do activities match your relative's interests and abilities?	☐	☐
○ Do staff do activities with residents 1:1 as well as in groups?	☐	☐
○ Are there volunteers who assist with activities?	☐	☐

Meals

Be sure to mention if your relative has a special diet – gluten intolerant, vegetarian, lactose intolerant, etc.

	YES	NO
○ Can my relative's diet be accommodated?	☐	☐
○ What times are meals served?		
○ Do residents have a choice of what time to eat meals?	☐	☐
○ Is the dining room quiet or loud?		

If your relative is sensitive to noise and commotion, is there a quiet area for meals?

Medical Care

Larger assisted living homes commonly have a nurse on site for 1 or 2 shifts, typically the morning and afternoon shifts. Many smaller homes do not have a nurse on site, but some do.

	YES	NO
○ Can your relative's doctor treat her here?	☐	☐
○ Is there a medical director?	☐	☐
○ Are there nurses on staff?	☐	☐

If yes, when? How many days a week and what hours during the days?

○ What are the titles and credentials of the person(s) dispensing medications?

○ What is the procedure for notifying families about a change in a resident's medical condition, behavior or medication?

○ Who takes a resident to doctor appointments: staff or family?

Emergencies And End Of Life Care

Residential care homes will need information about who is the emergency contact. Many request copies of advance directives, Do No Resuscitate (DNR) orders or living wills for their files.

○ **How are emergencies handled? (E.g., falls, heart attacks, high fevers)**

○ **When is 911 automatically called?**

○ **If my relative has a Do Not Resuscitate (DNR) order, will it be honored?**

	YES	NO
Is the DNR shown to the Medical responders?		
At what point is the family called?	☐	☐

○ **What documents do I need to provide to make end of life decisions for my relative?**

	YES	NO
○ **Is Hospice care provided?**		
○ What end of life circumstances would require my relative to move out?	☐	☐

Family Support Programs

	YES	NO
○ **Is a family support group offered on-site?**	☐	☐
○ **Is there a social worker on staff?**	☐	☐
○ **Are family education groups offered?**	☐	☐
○ **Are there social events for families?**	☐	☐

Transitions in Dementia Care,©, 2019, Dementiacarebooks.com.

LAURIE WHITE AND BETH SPENCER

Additional Notes:

Made in the USA
Lexington, KY
05 May 2019